FOREX

TRADING

THE ULTIMATE BEGINNERS GUIDE TO LEARN FOREX TRADING. ALL YOU NEED TO KNOW TO GET STARTED AND MAKE MONEY ONLINE IN THE MOST PROFITABLE MARKET!

Table of Contents

INTRODUCTION

In simple terms, forex trading is a form of trade where traders buy and sell currencies. Traders forecast the value of one currency to another so that they can make a profit. The reason why they are traded in pairs is this. Unless you compare it with another currency, the value of one currency doesn't change.

In forex trading, you represent currency pairs as shown below:

- EUR/USD

The base currency is the first currency while the quote currency is the second currency. Why Forex trading?

There are many things that the Forex market has to offer. Some of them are listed below:

- **Accessibility.** Ever wondered why the Forex market has the largest trading volume? It's because of the level of accessibility that Forex market presents. All that you need to participate in forex is a computer with a stable internet connection.

- **Narrow focus.** The forex market has more than 8 major trading currencies. A small market means that there is little chance for confusion.

- **24-hour market.** If there is anything that you can count on in the forex market, it is open 24 hours daily.

- **Liquidity.** The major trading platform across the world is the forex market. High volumes of trade make it one of the best liquid market. This means that under normal market conditions, traders can still buy and sell currencies as they prefer.

- **Impossible to corner the market.** Since it is the largest platform, it's not easy for one to deceive the market.

CURRENCY PAIRS

There are very many types of currencies across the world, and all of them have three letter symbols, for example, the Euros are EUR, American Dollar are USD, British Pounds are GBP, Swiss Francs are CHF, etcetera. The currencies have been majorly divided into two major and minor currencies. The major currencies involve these derived from the powerful economies in the world that are; the USA, the UK, Japan, the Eurozone, Australia, Canada, New Zealand, and Switzerland. These currencies create forex pairs with each other and with other minor currencies.

When one goes to a store to purchase some groceries or any other item, he/she needs to exchange one asset of value for another for instance milk for money. This applies for forex exchange too; buying and selling one currency for another. Every pair involves two currencies whereby one buys or sells the currencies against the other.

Forex pairs can be classified into three types namely Major pairs, Exotic pairs, and Minor pairs. The major pairs always consist of the United States Dollar and many people trade in them. The major pairs are USDCHF, USDJPY, EURUSD, AUDUSD, GBPUSD, NZDUSD, and USDCAD. The minor pairs involve all the currencies participating in the major pairs apart from the United States Dollar. They include CHFJPY, EURGBP, EURAUD, JPYAUD, NZDCAD et cetera. The exotic pairs involve one minor currency and one major currency, for instance, USDNOK, USDKSH, EURTRY etcetera.

HOW DOES FOREX WORK?

Just like the stock markets, one can trade currencies depending on his/her prediction on the changes of value. The greatest difference between stocks and currency trades is that forex can trade down and up very easily. If one thinks that a particular currency will have a value increase, he/she may buy it, and if he thinks that the currency will fall, he /she may sell it. The forex market is so large that finding a buyer or seller is too easy compared to other trade markets. Let's assume that a trader hears reports that a country such as China will devalue its currency with the intention of drawing more foreign investors into the country. If he/she thinks that the devaluing trend will continue, the trader may sell the currency of China against another, for example, the USD. The more the currency of China devalues against the United States dollar, the higher the trader's profit. However, if the currency gains value against the US dollar, then the trader will have increased losses and may want to leave the trade as soon as possible.

Summarily, Forex trading involves placing a bet on the value of one currency against the other. Remember that in a pair, the first currency is the base while the second currency is the secondary or the counter. For example, in the EUR/USD the EUR is the base while the USD is the counter. If a trader clicks buy or sell, he/she is buying or selling the base. This means that if a forex trader thinks that the EUR will increase in value in contrast with the United States dollar, he/she will buy the EURUSD. If the trader thinks that it will drop, he/she will sell the EURUSD. If for instance the asking price 0.7060 and the bid price is 0.7064, and then the spread price is 4 pips. Whether the value of the EUR rises or falls, the trader will make a profit or loss once he covers the spread price. The spread price is usually higher for minor currencies.

BASIC TERMS IN FOREIGN EXCHANGE

In foreign exchange, the term 'Position' refers to a trade that is in progress, and it is basically classified according to the expectation of traders. The term 'long position' refers to the trade where the trader has purchased a particular Currency (the first in a pair) with the expectation that the value will rise. When the trader sells back the currency to the market (expected to be a higher price than the purchase price), the trade is complete, and the long position is "closed." A short position refers to the trade where a trader sells a currency (the first in a pair) with the expectation that the value will fall and then he/she buys it back at a lower price. When the trader buys the currency back ideally for less than he/she sold it the trade is complete, therefore "closed."

The pair that is mainly traded in the forex market is the American dollar versus the Euro or USDEUR. The currency identified on the left side is referred to as the Base currency, while the one on the right is referred to as secondary currency. The base currency is the one a buyer or seller wishes to buy or sell while the secondary currency is the one a trader uses to make the transaction. Each trade pair has two prices, the bid, and the buy. The 'bid' is the selling price of the base currency while the 'ask' is the buying price. The difference between the bid and the asking price is referred to as the spread, and it indicates the amount that brokers charge to keep the position open. The spreads become narrower when more currency is traded that is when a currency has high volatility. If a pair is very rare, the spread will be wider.

Usually, the quote prices are presented with 4 numbers after the dot. In the case of EURUSD for example, the price might be 1.2589 to mean that for every Euro that a trader wishes to buy, he/she will have to put in 1.2589 US dollars. Changes occurring in the value of the currency will be seen on the last figure after the dot. It is mainly referred to as a pip. The gains, the loses, and the spreads will normally be indicated in pips. Another term commonly used in forex trading is going long which means buying and going short means selling. A bullish trader normally predicts that the market will rise while the bearish trader hopes that the market will fall to benefit. The term bull market indicates that the market will rise or increase while the bear market indicates that the market will fall or decrease. Experienced traders normally base their decisions and strategies on the market trends; therefore, they follow all the relevant events within the markets. The study of trends helps the traders to gain profit in the market.

Formally, traders had to call the brokers and inform them of the actions he/she should take in the market. However, technology has made it possible for many traders to transact directly using software referred to as a trading platform. There are many trading platforms available for the internet, computers and even phones. Every trader selects a platform that will work well with his/her trade strategy to reap maximum benefits.

Leveraged trading, also referred to as trading on the margin is a process that allows the traders to hold larger positions than he/she can with his own fortune only. In a large number of forex pairs, a trader can hold maximum leverage of 400:1 which means that for every $400 the trader will invest $1. Consequently, if he/she wishes to purchase 100000 of EURUSD at the price of 1.2674, instead of paying $126,740 he/she will pay 25 percent for the amount. One should remember that the losses and profits usually depend on the size of the position and as much as leveraging trade can magnify the profits, it can also enhance losses.

Example

Let's say a trader wants to transact in the forex market. He/she logs onto the trading platform and checks the bid and ask price. Assuming that he/she finds that the asking price is 1.2356 and the bid price is 1.2359; the pip will be 1.2356-1.2359= 3 pips. The three pips will go to brokers. If for instance, that trader believes that the Euro will rise, he will put a 'buy' command. He will then select a particular amount of units he/she wishes to buy for instance 10,000. The normal price for that would be $12356 and if the trader is relying on leverage trading, he will pay$30.89. If the markets move up as the trader had indicated, say to $1.2360, then he/she will make a profit.

Chapter1 : THE PRINCIPLES OF FOREX MARKET

As said earlier, the forex market is one of the biggest platforms across the world. There are many trading opportunities in the forex market because it can make a much higher profit than in the stock market.

You can Trade in Forex 24-hours a day

Financial markets open in New Zealand, Japan, Pacific, and other Asian countries at 5 pm ET on Sunday. By the time the above markets start to close, the Middle East and European market start to open. So, other forex markets across America open when Europe is in mid-season. The pattern continues until 5 pm ET on Friday when Forex markets in America close. In this case, traders have about 5.5 days per week to trade.

Who can trade in Forex?

Anyone can trade in Forex as long as you have the starting capital and some knowledge about forex markets. Also, if you don't have enough capital, big financial organizations lend small and medium-sized traders money to use in the forex market. However, you must prove that you are knowledgeable in forex trading.

Currencies to Trade

With forex, the basis of your trading currency will be the offered currency pairs of your dealer. However, since it is your first time to trade, you should stick with the eight major currencies.

 Pips, Lots, and Leverage

So far, you know something about forex trading: you know when to trade it, who can trade it, and some of the currencies available. This section reviews some of the key concepts that you should be familiar with before you trade your first pair of currency. Typically, in the forex trading, you will see that the prices of currency pairs are shown in 5 decimal places. However, some currency is shown in two decimal places like the Japanese Yen. Regardless of the type of currency you're using to trade, the last big number behind the decimal is the pip. A pip is the leading unit price that can you change for the currency pair. When trading, you measure your profits and losses in pips. Sometimes, there is a smaller number that comes after the pip. This number is called a fractional pip. A fractional pip shows the exact price. You'll find cases where the fractional pip is 0. That means there is no fractional pip. A single unit of movement represents one pip. To some people, this is small, and it may make them question how one can make a high profit in forex if what a trader is speculating is just a fraction of a currency. However, that should not worry you at all. Many people trade in forex around the world, and so when you add all the small fractions, it increases in size.

What is a lot?

In simple terms, a lot is a standard unit of measurement. A single standard lot is equivalent to 100, 000 worth of currency. In some forex trading platforms, you are allowed to trade at intervals of 1,000 units. However, there is no need to invest $1,000 because you have the leverage to use to trade.

Leverage

The best thing with forex trading is the ability to use leverage.

Many forex traders consider the leverage offered by forex dealers interesting. However, it is important to mention that trading using this approach can be risky. The same way it can produce significant profits is the same way it can result in significant losses.

How leverage, lots, and pips work in forex?

Let's assume that you have purchased 10, 000 EUR/ USD on 50:1. You bought 1.3000o and closed the trade by selling 1.3020o. So you have made 20 pips.

Now, 0.0001 x US$10,000 = US$1 per pip

Now, a 20 pip trade gives you US$20.

Remember that not all pips are worth US$1. The value of a pip is determined by the size of the lot in the trade, the currency pair, the number of lots traded on, and the accuracy of the account.

While this calculation can be done with an online pip calculator, most trading applications automatically compute pip values and convert to the currency a trader is trading on.

Chapter 2: FOREX TERMINOLOGY

As with most specialized areas, the Forex market comes with its own terminology that can be utterly undecipherable to the uninitiated. Before we discuss how to trade in Forex, let's get you acquainted with those words and phrases to help you navigate the information more easily.

- **Ask Price**: This is the price that a seller is willing to accept for a trade on the market.

- **Spread**: This is the difference between the bid and ask price and is where the broker makes their money. The more volatility in the market, the wider the spread is likely to be.

- **Exchange Rate**: A familiar term for vacationers, this refers to the value of one currency in terms of another. For instance, how many Euros you would get for one Australian dollar.

- **Currency Pairs**: The Forex market does not deal with individual currencies, but with pairs of them. For example, the U.S. dollar combined with the Canadian dollar. Some are much more widely traded than others.

- **Cross Currency**: A trade in which neither currency is the U.S. dollar.

- **Cross Rate**: A currency exchange rate between two currencies in which neither are the official currency of the country in which that rate is given. For instance, if an American publication quoted an exchange rate for the Canadian dollar and the Japanese yen.

- **G7 and G20**: These seven countries – the United States, Italy, Japan, France, Germany, Canada and the United Kingdom – are the countries with the most major economic developments and represent over two thirds of the world's wealth. Their currencies are stable, creating currency pairings that have high volume and volatility. The G20 includes these countries but also others including China, India, Argentina, Australia, South Africa, South Korea, Mexico, Saudi Arabia, Turkey, Brazil and the European Union. These together make up four fifths of the world's trade and 85 percent of the gross domestic product on the planet. These currencies are the ones you will focus on as a trader.

- **Restricted Currencies**: Some governments do not allow trading or speculation with their currencies. This can be because there is a limited availability, concern about the effect of speculation or a desire to control foreign investment.

- **Pip**: This refers to the smallest possible increment by which a currency can move in price. Some currencies are quoted to four or five decimal places, so a pip refers to 0.0001 or 0.00001 of that pound, franc or Euro. Others are quoted only to two decimal places, so a pip is 0.01.

- **Volume**: In Forex trading, this refers to the number of units being traded at one time. One currency may only have five or ten transactions taking place on it over the course of a day, while another may have thousands upon thousands. The former therefore has a low volume of trade, while the latter has a high volume.

- **Volatility**: This refers simply to how much change there is in the trading price of a currency over time. The most that price changes, the more volatile that currency is said to be.

- **Margin**: If you don't have enough money to invest in a trade, you can get a secured loan from your broker to increase your capital. This is known as using margin. Doing so involves a great deal of risk as, if the trade is not successful, you will find yourself in significant debt.

- **Margin call**: This term refers to your broker requiring you to settle your account, usually when a trade reaches a certain level of risk.

Chapter 3: RISK MANAGEMENT AND TYPES OF RISKS

A trader can have the best trading system for the forex market, but without a good risk management plan, one could lose everything in a matter of hours. In the simplest term, risk management involves putting together ideas that offer downside protection for traders. In the foreign exchange market, a trader can opt for a number of strategies including selecting an appropriate loss size, using stop-loss orders, diversifying the investment, and using analysis tools to monitor the trades.

RISKS MANAGEMENT TIPS

Apart from stop-loss orders and diversification, there are a number of tips that one may follow to reduce risk including:

Make the trend a companion

One may have decided to hold a position for an extended time. However, every trader should recognize that no matter the position they take, there is no fighting against the market trends and movements. Accommodate the changes and make sure that the trading strategies reflect the new aspects; this will help one to reduce risk.

Keep learning

There is always new information coming up in the market every day. As the world changes, so does the economy and so does the market. A trader should know how the market is currently functioning, how it evolved and where it might be heading.

Use tools and software programs

Use of tools and programs can help one select a good choice and avoid risk. However, it is important to note that these systems are man-made therefore aren't entirely perfect. It is best to use them as a tool of advice rather than a complete basis of trading decisions.

Use limited leverage

Leveraging is very attractive because it gives a trader the opportunity to make bigger profits. However, leverage also increases the chances of losing capital; therefore, one should avoid taking massive leverage. One wrong move with leverage and the entire account is wiped out.

Forex risk management involves a lot of aspects that are actually very easy to understand. Most of them have been covered in this book. The hard part is to summon enough self-discipline to follow the rules when the market is dictating otherwise. The bottom line is, when a trader limits risk, he/she is able to stay in the game for longer and continue investing even under adverse conditions.

Chapter 4: TRADING PSYCHOLOGY

Psychology and trading, most people might think that these factors don't relate to one another. Well, it very well does. As I mentioned earlier, most trading mistakes occur because the traders don't understand the importance of trading psychology. However, most traders don't trade successfully, mainly because of emotional problems. Especially, naïve traders don't handle emotions well, so they don't remain in the market for long. But, it is not something good which is why educating naïve traders is important. Even before they enter the market, it is important to spend the time to learn the market. However, the most common issue with trading is fear. But, fear is commonly seen when the trader moves into the live trading account. But, initially, the temptation is often found in naïve traders. When they enter the market, they enter with the thought of trading as much as possible to make money. Hence, this thought will not let them achieve what they actually should achieve. Therefore, when a trader is tempted to trade, he or she may trade even without analyzing or anticipating the trades.

However, as mentioned fear can also create a lot of issues in a trader's journey. Many traders give up trading completely because of fear. But, the fight or flight reaction is a human thing, that is commonly seen in traders. But actually, this reaction cannot be changed that easily, but of course, traders can handle this reaction wisely. If you study trading psychology, things will become simpler when trading the Forex market. Anyway, when you fear to trade, it will impact your trading behaviors negatively. Most of the time, you will look for a safer method to trade and, perhaps, it is not possible to find safer trading methods in the Forex market.

As you already know, the Forex market involves a lot of risks, so as traders, you must learn to handle them carefully. For example, when you enter into a trade, your instincts point out the chances of losing and you will eventually exit from the trade, and it might have been a profitable trade. So see, your mind has a direct connection to the way you trade.

Even if you have a defined plan, you can still steer away from trading because the power of psychology is immense. You might even become anxious and consider short-term positions because you are afraid to enter into long-term positions even if they seem profitable. Well, yes, fear, greed, and all the other emotions can cause a lot of problems to your trading journey. Hence, you must understand trading psychology. If you do, you will be able to assist those emotions wisely and handle trading successfully. Normally, if you overcome fear, it will be beneficial to your trading journey as well as life.

Typically, traders don't fear the market when they are preparing to enter into a trade, but when the market opens, their emotions play the role. As humans, you can never get rid of emotions because it is a part of humankind. But, you can always learn the methods to control your emotions when excitement is a dangerous emotion when trading the Forex market. When you are excited, you might make mistakes when entering a trade or anticipating market movements. Thus, when you are trading, you have to try to keep your emotions neutral.

Most traders succumb to accept that they are making trading mistakes that are related to psychology. But normally, when people can't accept, denial is the first reaction. Over time, they tend to accept the truth. Just like that, even the naïve traders will learn to accept the truth. However, Forex trading is not only about trading system and strategies. You must accept that mindset is an important part of Forex trading. The way you anticipate the Forex market has a lot to do with trading. Also, only if you understand the trades will you be able to enter into it. Thus, a trader's mindset has a lot to do with trading.

If you look at certain websites that advertise robotic trading systems, you might find trading psychology as an absurd thing. But, remember, those trading systems will not provide benefits as they portray. Nothing is as best as trading manually. You must use your knowledge and skills to trade the market; only then will you be able to trade successfully. Also, those websites are doing their duty to market their product, and if you rely on them and purchase it, you might have to pay them for using their product. Hence, when you come across something like this, make sure to think logically. As a beginner, you must try to settle for a simple yet effective strategy, so that you will be able to trade peacefully.

Anyway, why do you think most naïve traders struggle to make money? You might have seen many people who fail in trading the Forex market. Well, there are many reasons why traders fail, but the major reason is the ones who enter the Forex market don't really know the market. A higher percentage of traders enter into the Forex market by believing the fabricated ads. And it makes them set unrealistic goals. Eventually, they struggle to meet those unrealistic goals and end up quitting trading. But the worst part is that there are traders who quit their day job after they enter the Forex market. Well, it is not a wise move because they must test to check whether trading works for them. Or some other traders believe trading is easy money and no matter how many times I repeat it, some people still believe it is possible. These thoughts create tension and stress, so eventually, the trader becomes emotionally unstable. Thus, when traders trade with an emotionally unstable mindset, they lose money.

So, how can a trader develop a trading mindset? If you want to develop a trading mindset, you need to do your part. It is important to put the required effort to accomplish what you are looking for. Well, you can't build a trading mindset that quickly because you have to learn and accept the Forex market as it is. If you try to deny facts about the Forex market, you will not be able to create a trading mindset.

You must start developing your trading mindset by handling the risks in trading. First of all, understand that risk management isn't for one trade, preferably it is applicable for all the trades that you enter into. You must make sure to calculate the risk for each trade before you enter into it. When you are managing risks, certain emotions might try to confuse you, but you must not let it happen. Once you start handling your emotions wisely, you will be able to manage trades also. However, the simplest way to control emotion when managing risks is to risk ONLY the amount that you can lose. You must create a mindset that enters into a trade while knowing the probability of losing trade. If you follow this, you will be able to remain in the trading world for a long time. But, it takes practice and patience to create a trading mindset that accepts losses. Also, you must master your trading edge. No matter what trading strategy you are using, you must know it completely to trade successfully.

And, remember, overtrading will never create profits. Instead, overtrading will blow all your hard-earned money. You must trade only when you actually see a profit signal. Don't try to trade just because you feel like trading. Or don't try to guess trade because that doesn't work in Forex trading. If you overtrade, it can be challenging to stop, and you'll become an emotional trader.

If you want to build a trading mindset, you must have an organized mindset. So, basically, when you have an organized mindset, you will think about the trading plan, journal, and much more. You must accept the fact that Forex trading is a business. Hence, don't try to gamble in the market. When you are making trading decisions, you must remain calm and steady; only then will you be able to think clearly.

But then, after you build a trading mindset, you must not let emotions play their role. However, the most common emotions that you must avoid are:

Euphoria

You might argue that euphoria is good, yes, it is good. But when it is related to the Forex market, it becomes dangerous. For example, if a trader wins a few profitable traders, he or she might become confident when trading the next trade. Well, it is good to feel confident when entering the next trade, but feeling overly confident is not a good thing. When traders become overly confident, they don't watch or study the market as they did before. The consecutive profitable trades should not get into your mind and increase the level of confidence. When trading Forex if you are overconfident, you will not be able to accept the loss if the trade doesn't react the way you wanted. Hence, it is better to remain calm even if you make profits continuously.

Fear

Most traders who enter the market with no knowledge about trading tend to fear the market. Also, some traders might fear because they cannot effectively trade using any specific strategy. However, usually, when a trader continuously experiences losses, he or she may tend to fear to trade. Perhaps, it is understandable because losing hard-earned money isn't easy. But, you can avoid the mistake of risking more than the amount that you are comfortable with. Most naïve traders don't follow this rule even if we keep repeating it. If fear persists, you will not be able to trade better trades or become successful. It has the power to keep you away from good trades as well. Hence, try to overcome fear by limiting the amount you risk in trading. For the naïve traders, start your journey on a demo account without directly entering the live account. If you do so, you'll be able to learn to control emotions.

Greed

You might have heard that people say only bulls and bears make money, but pigs get slaughtered. If you don't understand what it means, it means greed. If you are greedy, you will not be able to make money in the market. Instead, you will be kicked out of the market. Mostly, traders become greedy when they don't have self-discipline. Most traders make quick decisions when the market shows profitable trade signals, but it is not recommended. Instead, you must be calm and collected. Take some time to understand the market, focus on the risk ratio, set a plan, and then enter into the trade. Also, remember, if you are risking more than what you are ready to lose, it apparently shows your level of greed to make money. Thus, you must overcome greed if you don't want to lose your account.

Revenge

This is one of the funny behaviors of traders because what is the point in revenging the market? For the Forex market, you are just one amongst the millions, and it doesn't make sense. However, if you are trying to revenge trade just because you lost a few trades, remember, this might lead to further losses. When you are emotional, you will not be able to make wise decisions. Hence, you must wait for some time until your mind is stable and ready to trade.

So, when learning the psychology of trading, you might find it exciting. But, success can decide when you take these things into practice. You don't have to try these tips and ideas on the live account, instead use the demo account. The Forex market is one of the best markets because it has provided solutions for almost all the issues. So, as traders, if you solve your personal trading issues, you will be able to become a successful trader. But how to succeed in trading?

Chapter 5: PRINCIPLES AND CHARACTERISTICS OF CURRENCIES

Currency exchange has been in place for a long time now. And by a long time, we are not talking about a couple of hundred years or even a few thousand years. We are referring to the BC period. More specifically, to around 10,000 BC. The only difference was that at that time people used the barter system to exchange goods and services. But this created feelings of dissatisfaction among the traders. How can one gauge the value of objects? Even if they were referring to a specific object, how can they say that the object from one place is better than another? For example, let us assume that you were providing two bags of rice for a fine carpet. (I''m not sure if this was the exchange rate, but let's pretend that it is. Though if you are giving two bags of rice for a carpet, then that carpet better fly!) Now, you know that in your little village or town, carpets are of the finest quality. But does that mean all the carpets around the world have the same quality? Does that mean you are getting a fair return for your two bags of rice? Now imagine this scenario playing out between the countries. How can one set accurate values for each country's "currencies"? How can exchanges take place that are fair and governed by the right rules?

This situation created a system of bias and prejudice. This started to disrupt whatever form of economy was used during those times.

Eventually, the earliest coins were made in parts of what we now refer to as Turkey. Empires and nations around the world began to manufacture their own coins using precious materials like gold and silver.

This controlled the chaos of exchanges that took place between traders because everything had a proper value. If you are going to purchase something, you knew how much you had to pay for it.

Fast forward to the 19th century. More specifically, to the year 1847. Up until now, countries were commonly utilizing gold and silver to make international payments. But that changed with the introduction of the Gold Standard Monetary System. With this system in place, the paper currencies of the countries had a value directly linked to gold. This means that a certain value of money from a country could be converted into a specific amount of gold, depending on that country's currency value.

Over time, this system was dropped in order to give each country a degree of autonomy when managing their affairs. This means that each country is responsible for creating their own currencies without leveraging it against anything. When governments began issuing their own paper currencies that were not attached to a physical commodity like gold or silver, that currency was given the term "fiat money".

Why is this significant? As we had seen, autonomy.

But once again, what does this actually mean?

With the presence of fiat money, the value of the money is dependant on the relationship between the supply and demand of the country along with the stability of the government. Rather than using gold and silver to decide the value of the money, the situation of the country would derive the value of the money.

Enter World War II.

And once again, it started with chaos.

The whole world was experiencing unprecedented levels of chaos. Governments were scrambling to find a solution to stabilize the economies of the world. They turned their eyes to the U.S. dollar.

In order to provide a solution, the Bretton Woods Agreement was established. According to this agreement, the U.S. dollar was set as the exchange rate for gold, giving nations around the world one currency to work with when managing international trades. Other currencies were eventually pegged against the U.S. dollar.

Once again, another solution to control the chaos of exchanges was formed. But did it last? Sadly, no.

History has a strange habit of repeating itself. Because even the Bretton Woods Agreement became obsolete as it became apparent that countries progressed at different speeds. In fact, it was observed that new rules introduced in countries could change trade laws and currency values.

In 1971, the Bretton Woods Agreement was dropped. The world needed a different system of currency valuation.

The U.S. was once again placed in the pilot seat and with the country's guidance, a free-floating market was introduced that would actually determine the **exchange value** of currencies based on the demand and supply in a particular country.

Of course, this innovative way of looking at currencies brought with it a whole new set of problems, the most prominent being the fact that it was not always easy to establish fair exchange rates. Additionally, gathering information about a country and its governmental policies, domestic situations, and trade policies could not be done quickly enough.

Then came the 1990s, a time we should all be thankful for. After all, it was because of the internet boom that we now have access to Facebook, online multiplayer RPGs, Netflix, and YouTube.

One of the greatest achievements of the internet was the availability of information instantly to anyone, anywhere in the world. The foundation provided by the internet allowed people to create new and innovative technologies.

These innovations led to the establishment of various trading platforms.

As we saw earlier, prior to the availability of trading platforms, the Forex market was simply something only certain entities or individuals with high net worth could access. It was never really available to everyone and the thought of joining it probably meant you had to have a million dollars, take a loan, perform an ancient ritual to the god of money, and maybe even sacrifice a few goats.

It was like a realm that everyone wanted to be in but no one had any access to.

But trading platforms changed all that. Because of these platforms, there was a paradigm shift in the way people approached the Forex market.

This brings us to the concept of institutional and retail trading.

INSTITUTIONAL VS. RETAIL TRADING

In the world of trading, there are basically two forms of traders: institutional and retail. The difference between them dictates the way they approach their trades. For example, institutional traders usually make large trades as compared to retail traders. But what are they exactly?

Their names might just give you a clue as to what you can understand about them.

Retail traders refers to individual traders. These traders can be anyone in the world who has the ability to get in on a trade. On the other hand, institutional traders are those who represent large financial institutions, hedge funds, banks, or other big firms that manage money. You could say that institutional traders are "corporate" traders whereas retail traders are "home" traders.

So does the amount invested in the trade dictate the type of trader one becomes? Is that the only point of distinction?

Not quite.

Analysis

A retail trader usually prefers to use some sort of technical analysis system for their trades. They utilize price patterns and behaviors in the past or indicators in the present that dictate future price scenarios. On the other hand, institutional traders do not usually refer to only technical patterns or systems to show them opportunities in their trade.

Focus

As institutional traders have been dealing with the system for a long time, their experience has led them to hone their skills well. They make use of market sentiments and fundamentals. They make use of trading psychology (which is a firm grasp on their emotions and keeping an analytical mind despite the situation) and understanding of overall responses towards a currency. They are keeping a close eye on the news to see if there are certain trends or reactions that they can pick up on.

Retail traders are not experienced in managing risks or having a proper psychological mind for trading. However, this is a situation that happens to everyone who gets started in Forex trading. No one can be prepared for what they will experience. They have to experience it first before they can decide how to keep their minds sharp.

Leverage

Institutional traders do not usually use leverage. Their main attention is spent on risk management. Even if a situation were to occur where they had to make use of leverages, they would be careful about how much leverage they are going to use.

On the other hand, retail traders make the mistake of looking for brokers that provide them with high leverages. While that act in itself is not wrong, it does pose a problem to those retailers who choose their brokers solely on the criteria of how much leverage those brokers provide them.

Now that we have understood more about the Forex market and its players, it is time we look at the most essential component of the market, currencies. More importantly, we are going to look at some of the major players in the Forex market.

Chapter 6: CROSS CURRENCIES

US Dollar (USD)

To this day, the United States dollar remains the world's most important currency. This is particularly true in Forex. The strength of the US dollar has proven itself to be formidable, despite having gone through a lot of financial roadblocks instigated by local and global turmoil. The strength of the currency can be attributed to the country's continued economic strength. The United States has the largest economy, and the country does possess an abundant and liquid capital. Aside from its economy, the strength of the country's currency can also be attributed to its role in the global stage and might of its political and military presence.

The movements of all other currencies still pivot around the market's perception of the US dollar, making it the fulcrum of the Forex market. The US dollar is the most liquid amongst the other currencies, making it the only option to become the world's reserve currency. Around 65 percent of the world's reserves are in US dollars. Due to this fact, central banks around the world now choose to hold a massive amount of this particular currency within their ledgers.

Investors and businesses also regard the US dollar as the go-to safe currency. This has been proven during different global financial situations. During the global credit crisis in 2009, which caused the Lehman Brothers and Bear Stearns to go bankrupt, the US dollar actually appreciated in value. Investors who were fearful for the worst moved their assets to US government securities, which resulted in the currency's value increase. While most may not agree that treasury bonds are the safest location, what is important to note is that the US dollar is perceived as the safest investment in the world. As of the moment, the US dollar remains at the top in the Forex markets.

Euro (EUR)

While being relatively new on the global financial scene, the euro is currently the second most important currency in the Forex market. The currency was introduced in 1999 and officially entered circulation in 2002. The euro was meant to centralize the currencies of the different European countries, which mostly had their own currencies. Due to the proximity of the nations belonging to the European Union, a solution had to be made to eliminate unnecessary currency conversions. Over the years, it has completely replaced other sovereign currencies, including most recently the French franc and the Deutsche mark.

The euro is currently valued higher than a US dollar, and it has been able to keep it that way since it was introduced. The euro has also much appreciated in value by more than 70 percent since 2002. Investors and traders who bet big on its rise certainly made a lot of profit during that time. Over the years, a lot of confidence has also been put on the currency, making it a good alternative. Similar to other currencies, the euro has had its own share of ups and downs, particularly during the global credit crisis in 2008. The euro peaked at US$1.60 during that year. The global credit crisis wreaked havoc on the European banking system. The situation got worse, and the European Central Bank had to intervene. Several members of the European Union were on the verge of bankruptcy. Portugal, Ireland, Greece, and Spain all received financial support from the IMF and the European Union to avoid defaulting on their debt.

Japanese Yen (JPY)

The Japanese yen has been one of the most successful stories in modern foreign exchange. Japan's recovery after World War II saw it emerge as a formidable economic force on the world stage. Since the yen's introduction to the work market, it has grown by a staggering 400 percent against the US dollar. The rise started with the initial economic boom in Japan and is continuing up to this day. Japan is currently one of the world's second-largest economies, and it was holding that position until China overtook it.

The growth of the Japanese yen has unfortunately halted by the early 1990s. However, it has managed to stay at the same relative value. Price inflation in the country has not been a problem in the country, partly thanks to its sophisticated financial system. Japan currently has one of the largest debts in work, on a per-capita basis, but it continues to enjoy healthy demand for its currency. The country continues to attract large investments from all over the world. The performance of the Japanese yen and the country itself is quite impressive given that it does not have a lot of natural resources. The country mostly gets its commodities and energy needs from other nations.

In the last decade, the value of the yen had slightly declined. This was mainly caused by extremely low-interest rates in Japan, which some investors had taken full advantage of by taken out loans and making investments abroad. The decline was halted when investors decided to let go of their short bets on the currency.

British Pound (GBP)

The British pound, or the pound sterling, is currently the fourth-most-traded currency. Prior to the rise of the US Dollar, it was the strongest currency in the world. The strength of the British pound can be attributed to the fact that London remains to be the preeminent currency trading center in the world. Post-World War II, the British pound had gone through quite the fluctuations. Most of the dips can be attributed to the country's continually rising inflation and unemployment levels. The country's housing market is also nowhere near as robust as other countries. The United Kingdom's debt is also quite substantial, and its decision to print more money only made it worse. Like other currencies, the British pound dropped significantly during the 2008 financial crisis.

Swiss Franc (CHF)

Switzerland is amongst the wealthiest countries in the world, and its economy is robust and has proven itself to be very stable. Due to this fact, the Swiss franc has become the go-to currency for those looking for an excellent place to store their finances. The economy's stability is mostly thanks to the country's trade surplus and its profitable exports. This includes the export of highly-valuable jewelry such as expensive Swiss watches, tobacco products, chemicals, and manufacturing equipment. Switzerland also mostly evaded the effects of the global credit crisis thanks to the Swiss National Bank's decision to refrain from printing money.

Similar to the US dollar, the Swiss franc is a safe-haven currency. Some would even argue that it performs better than the US dollar in this regard. In fact, during times of global financial uncertainty, the value of the Swiss franc typically increases more than the other "safe" currencies. As for its movement in the Forex market, the Swiss franc closely mirrors the movement of the euro. This is mostly due to the close relationship with the Swiss and the Eurozone economies. However, the currency's value does deviate in times of political strife, thanks mainly to the country's neutrality in global political issues.

Australian Dollar (AUD)

While it might not sound correct, the Australian dollar is actually one of the strongest commodity currencies in the market. Its movement is closely tied to the movement of global commodity prices. This is mainly since the country is one of the world's largest producers of iron ore, coal, and other precious metals. The country's economy has so far taken advantage of China's growing demand for energy and basic commodities. Thanks to this, the country's economy was really damaged by the recent global financial crisis. Due to its close trade relationship with Asian countries, especially China, the Australian dollar's movement does somewhat mirror that of the Chinese yuan. In fact, some investors even treat the currency as a good proxy for the Chinese yuan.

Canadian Dollar (CAD)

The Canadian dollar is another commodity currency that is closely related to global commodity prices. The country is a large producer of energy commodities such as petroleum, timber, and coal. It also exports a number of agricultural products to different parts of the world. The Canadian dollar took advantage of the commodities boom in the mid-2000s and gained in 2010 where its value equaled that of the US dollar. This was the very first time that the Canadian dollar reached parity with the US dollar in over 30 years. Canada's economy is greatly dependent on that of the United States. Canada produces oil, electricity, and natural gas for the United States, which purchases around 75 percent of what the country produces. When the United States experiences a downtrend in its economy, the Canadian dollar swiftly follows.

Other Currencies

There are currently around 180 legal currencies that are circulating throughout the world. Amongst those currencies, only a handful are actively traded on the Forex market. Most Forex brokers trade between 40 to 70 currency pairs, with some trading more than others. Aside from the currencies mentioned above, there are a few currencies that have become recently significant. This includes the New Zealand dollar, which is closely influenced by the movement of the Australian dollar. The New Zealand dollar is also greatly reliant on the prices of global commodities. The country is a large producer of agricultural products and dairy-based items. The Chinese Yuan has also recently gained prominence, thanks to the rapid growth of the country's economy. It is arguably a currency that investors should look out for given its sudden emergence into the world stage. China has the second largest economy in the world, and it is one of the biggest international traders out there. The Chinese Yuan is pinned to the US dollar.

Apart from the major currencies mentioned above and the recent ones that have gained prominence, all of the other currencies are considered to be exotic currencies. These currencies are also sometimes referred to as emerging market currencies; mostly due to their association with their respective country's emerging economies. These economies tend to have large fluctuations in the market, mostly due to high inflation and significant political and economic changes. In some cases, some of these currencies can rise to unprecedented levels when times are good. However, these are also the currencies that drop the most during times of crisis. Some of the more popular exotic currencies that are traded in the Forex market include the Korean won (KRW), Turkish lira (TRY), the Russian ruble (RUB), the Indian rupee (INR), the Brazilian real (BRL) and the South African Rand (ZAR). Along with seven other exotic currencies, these emerging currencies account for a combined 9 percent overall trade volume in the Forex market.

Currency Pairs

Among the 160 different currencies circulating in different parts of the world, there are only handfuls that are actively exchanged in the Forex market. Most of them are only exchanged in the territories where they are used. The current Forex market actively trades in only around 17 currencies based on their liquidity and the number of exchanges made between those currencies. These so-called major currencies account for over 90 percent of all the money exchanged in the foreign currency exchange market.

Similar to company stocks in the stock market, currencies are assigned three-letter abbreviations, set by the International Standards Organization. This greatly simplifies the quoting and trading of these currencies in the world market. When trading these currencies, the quote for these trades is always shown in pairs. Each currency fluctuates relative to other currencies, which is why they are traded in pairs. Out of the active major currencies, there are hundreds of potential currency combinations. However, there are about 100 pairs that are commonly traded, with around 50 pairs actively being used by international Forex brokers.

In Forex trading, exotic currencies are generally paired with major currencies. It is doubtful that a non-major currency will be paired with another non-major currency. As an example, it would be challenging to find an exchange that trades the Uruguay Peso and the Iraqi dinar. However, finding an exchange that trades those currencies with the US dollar is relatively easy. Some companies and individuals do exotic trade pairs with another, but their volume merely is just too small for international brokers.

Currency Quotations

The International Organization for Standardization submitted ISO 4217 in 1978. The standard assigned three-letter codes to represent individual currencies to be used in any application for trading, banking, and commerce. It was also agreed upon that the three-letter alphabetic codes for International Standard ISO 4217 would be used in international trading. The list of codes is also frequently updated, as new currencies emerge and older ones are discontinued.

When it comes to Forex trading, currencies always come in pairs. As an example, a trade made with the US dollar versus the euro would look like this (USD/EUR). The US dollar versus the Canadian dollar would look like this (USD/CAD). It goes without saying that a currency can never be traded without itself.

The first currency indicated in the quotation is called the base currency, while the second one is referred to as the counter currency. A numerical value is assigned to the currency pair that may be up to 4 decimal places. The last decimal place is referred to as a "pip." The value assigned to currency pairs is the amount of the counter currency required to buy one unit of the base currency. As an example, if the USD/CAD is quoted at 1.32, it means that it would currently require 1.32 Canadian dollars to buy one single US dollar. On trading platforms, these values would fluctuate in real-time as the value of each currency varies depending on the market.

Chapter 7: OPENING A POSITION

Forex exchange has been around for very many years, and some say that it is as old as the invention of national currencies. Over the years, the market has grown so much so that it is the biggest market across the world. However, it has not been accessible to the public as easily as it is today. From the 1990s when the era of the internet begun, many retail forex brokers have established routes through which anyone can trade in currencies so long as they can access the internet and have some money. There is a lot of hype and information about forex trade on the internet, but not everybody understands how to select and open an account.

Currently, opening a forex account has become as easy as opening a bank account or another type of brokerage account. Some of the typical requirements are a name, phone number, address, email, a password, account currency type, country of citizenship, date of birth, employment status, and tax ID or Social security number. Opening an account may also require one to answer some financial questions such as their net worth, annual income, trading objectives, and trading experience. Before one starts to trade on the foreign exchange market, they should make some considerations to ensure that they have a positive, secure and successful experience.

The right broker

The first step to trading well is to find the right broker. The activities of forex exchange are decentralized, and there are hardly any regulations. Because of the over the counter nature, traders are advised to identify a reliable broker. This involves conducting researches on the reputation of the broker; to identify if there is a history of irregular practices. One may also want to comprehensively understand the services offered by the particular broker before setting up an account. While some brokerages support basic and plain vanilla activities, others offer very sophisticated trading platforms. Some brokers will offer the trader analytical resources to support better decision making while others won't.

Again, a trader should assess the fees and commissions for different brokers. The majority of Brokers charge some fees for their services through the bid-ask spread and, in many cases, it is not a large percentage. However, some brokerages have some other fees and commissions, and they might be hidden from the trader. When one is considering the extra costs, he/she should check if it is worthwhile.

The procedure

Opening a foreign exchange account is not hard, but traders should have a few things in order to get started. The trader will have to provide some identification information such as name, phone number, country of origin et cetera. Besides, the trader will be required to state his/her trade intentions and their level of knowledge and experience in the trade. The steps of opening an account may vary depending on the brokerage firm, but normally it involves:

- Accessing the website of the broker and study the accounts available. The accounts include small ones where the trader can trade with minimum capital such as mini accounts or the sophisticated accounts designed for experienced traders such as standard trading account.
- Completing an application form,
- Getting registered (user name and password) in order to access the account.
- Log in to the client portal and arrange for a transfer of money from the bank to the forex account. These deposits can be made through credit or debit card, checks, or electronic transfers.
- Once the funds are transferred, the trader is ready to start trading. Before trading, the trader may review the recommendations made by the brokers or extra services offered such as simulator programs.

The use of margins

Once a trader has opened an account, he/she has to decide whether to apply a margin or not. A margin is a leverage move whereby the broker offers the trader a loan in order to increase the available capital. A broker can offer a margin on capital for any rate between 50:1 and 400:1 depending on the country they operate from. The amount that a trader wants in terms of margin will determine the amount of capital that he/she will deposit in the account. The deposit acts as collateral for the trading activities. True, margins increase potential profits, but one should be warned that they also increase the risks. In case of loss, the trader will be required to cover the costs even if they are beyond the initial investment.

Chapter 8: PIPS, MICROS, MINIS, LOTS

The forex market is highly liquid due to the high demand and supply rate. The traders usually transact based on general events as well as financial events. Under normal circumstances, when a currency has high demand, its value rises in comparison with other currencies, and if the demand is low, then the value will fall.

Financial Events

Financial events refer to the statements made by different countries, central banks, and other financial institutions on subject matters such as manufacture numbers, unemployment rate, loan interest rates et cetera. If a country makes a statement that the unemployment rate has dropped, people might interpret it as a stronger economy; therefore, the value of the local currency will increase. If the currency of the country among the major ones, it will most probably affect other currencies. Before an event occurs, whether general or financial, the traders speculate about the contents and expected changes and open positions based on their predictions.

Lot Size

A lot is defined as the minimum available trade size that a trader can place in the market of Foreign exchange. Generally, brokers refer to lots in calibrations of one thousand or a micro lot. One should note that the lot size has a direct impact on the risk taken. As such, a trader can use tools like risk management calculators to identify the most appropriate lot size based on the size of his/her account. These tools can also help the trader to understand the amount he/she is willing to risk. The size of a lot that one takes has a large impact on how much every market move will affect his/her account. This means that a 100 pip move on a small position (trade size) will not affect the account as much as the same 100 pips on a large position. In the forex trade market, there are different lot sizes that one can trade in for instance Mini lots, micro lots, and standard lots.

Micro Lots

The smallest tradable lot in the forex exchange available for most traders and brokers is the micro lots. A micro lot includes one thousand units of the currency used to fund the account. If the account is funded in United States dollars, then a micro lot is equal to 1000 USD of the base currency one wants to trade in. If a trader is trading a pair that is based on dollars, then one pip would equal to 10 cents. Micro lots are handy for beginner traders because they help one feel more at ease while trading.

Mini Lots

Before the micro lots were introduced, the market had mini lots whereby each mini lot equaled to ten thousand (10000) units of the account funding currency. If for instance, a trader is dealing with a dollar-based account like in the illustration given above, then each pip move in a trade will be worth about one dollar. If a trader wants to start trading through the mini lots, he/she should be well capitalized.

One pip equaling to $1 seems like a very small amount to cover all the risk in forex trading. However, the market is highly volatile; therefore, it can move even to 100 pips a day equaling to $100. In some cases, these movements can happen even in less than an hour. A trader should also remember that if the market moves against him/her in the above case scenario, the loss will be equal to $100. It is up to the trader to decide their ultimate risk tolerance levels, but the best option for a trade venturing in the mini lots is to start with a minimum of $2000 in order to be comfortable.

Standard Lots

A standard lot refers to a 100k unit lot. If a trader is trading in dollars, a standard lot is equal to 100,000 units. Normally, the average pip size in the case of standard lots is ten us dollars. A very important aspect that a trader should note while dealing with standard pips is that 10 pips down is the same as 100 us dollars loss. Standard lots are best suited for institutional-size accounts. As such, one has to have at least $25000 in order to make standard lot trades.

Many of the individual forex traders stay in the micro and mini lots, and although it does not look like it makes much money, a good trading plan will ensure long term survival. To help you understand the impact of a lot size on an account, let us look at an example. Let's say you are walking across a valley on a rope bridge that seems quite strong and stable. So long as your weight can be supported by the bridge, you have very little to worry about even if a storm ensued or a gushing wind started rocking the bridge. However, if you are carrying a sizeable backpack and luggage, when the storm kicks in, you have to be worried because the bridge might not be strong enough. The larger the burden, the more the risk: keep in mind that the strength of the bridge is not being adjusted.

The same case applies to forex trade lot size. If one selects a small trade size compared to his/her account, then it is like walking over a safe bridge with little disturbances. Even if the market moves, it will hardly affect the capacity of the trader. However, if a trader selects a large trade size compared to the size of the account, then the bridge might not withstand the weight, a slight change in the conditions could send the trader to a land of no return.

Determining a position size in the forex trade

In forex trading, the trade size or the position size has more significance than the timing. A trader may have the best entry and exit strategy, but if he/she does not know the size of a trade or position, he/she may take either too much risk or too little risk. Taking too much risk should raise a concern because it might evaporate an account too quickly. The position refers to the number of lots a trader takes in each trade (Micro, mini or standard). The risk is normally classified into two parts namely account risk and trade risk. These elements work together to give the trader an ideal position regardless of the market conditions, the current trade setup or the strategy that one is using.

The first step to determining a position in the foreign exchange trade is to set an account risk limit. One sets the risk limit according to the amount of capital they are willing to lose. Many experienced traders risk a maximum of 1 percent per trade. For instance, if a trader has $10000, then he/she may risk $100 at the risk rate of 1 %. The risk limit can also be set in dollar amounts instead of percentages. With a set account risk limit, all the variables affecting the market may change, but the risk remains constant. It is better if a trader identifies one account risk percentage or amount and applies it in all the trades.

The second step involves identifying pip risk. A trader should turn all the attention to the trade and calculate the difference between the place where they placed the stop order and the entry point. Remember that a stop loss order closes a trade if it loses a certain amount that is set by the trader. Stop loss order helps to keep the risk within the selected limits like the one mentioned earlier (1 percent). However, each trade has a different pip risk based on the strategy or volatility. In some cases, a trade may have 6 pips while another had 16 pips.

When a trader is making a trade, he/she should consider his/her entry point and the stop loss location. It is best to have the stop loss as close to the entry point as possible. However, the trader should ensure that the stop loss is not too close to the entry point to the extent of stopping the trade before the expected move occurs. Once a person knows the difference between the entry point and the stop loss, he/she will be able to calculate the deal position for the trade.

The third step involves determining the position size for Trade. The ideal position can be calculated using a simple mathematical formula; Pip value * pip risk * lots traded is equal to $ at risk. From the first step, we identified the $ at risk, and this is the maximum amount of money that one can risk. In the second step, we identified the pips at risk.

Chapter 9: UNDERSTANDING CHART

We have been talking about how you should refer to charts when you are conducting your Forex transactions. But that begs the question, is there Forex software that will meet your needs and at the same time provide you with tons of features?

The satisfying answer is that there is!

That software is TradingView.

Let's start with a brief summary of what TradingView is all about.

So what exactly is the TradingView?

It is convenient charting software that also provides traders with the ability to network on the platform. TradingView is ideal for all kinds of trades, whether they are beginners or veterans. It is meant to provide you with a visual representation your trading (which is what we want after all) and supplements that view with tons of information about the trade.

Here are some of the cool features of the software:

Depending on how you would like to approach your trade, you can create simple charts or complex dynamic and multi-layered charts to track a plethora of markets.

Additionally, if you feel like it, you can even create your own charts on the platform.

The software comes with different kinds of alerts that you can modify on the platform. Based on what kind of information you require urgent updates about, you can adjust up to 12 different notification settings.

For those who have honed their skills in charting software, TradingView also provides the feature of "Pine Script". What this script allows you to do is create your indicators and charts.

The platform also gives you access to over 50 exchanges around the world, enough to fulfill all your trading needs.

Finally, to add the cherry on the cake, TradingView provides a lot of educational materials. They have everything from videos to podcasts to articles giving you details on how you can trade and how you can manage finances, to how you should be looking at the various charts. Simply put, you have all the information you need to get started on the platform and become acclimated to the Forex world.

You can sign up for a free account, but it is not necessary to view some of the information on the platform. If you would like to simply make a quick reference, then head over to TradingView and you will spot a ticker on the top of the website giving you updates about the popular currency pairs.

MOBILE CHARTING PLATFORMS

Today's world is all about going mobile. If you have a business, it has become vital to target mobile users. It is for this reason that platforms such as Facebook, Google, YouTube, and Instagram all have special marketing campaigns that target mobile users.

In the same way, there are numerous mobile versions of charting platforms that you can access from anywhere in the world, as long as you are connected to a network.

But out of all the platforms available to you, which ones are actually worth looking into? Here are the ones you should consider if you are going to work on charts.

Netdania

One of the highlights of this app is that it provides you with trading strategies and ideas. The creators of the app have marketed the platform as a "personal trading assistant" and in many ways, it does function that way. For example, the app actually gives you a notification to let you know when the right time to go long or go short is. While doing this, it accumulates real-time news and economic information from around the world. Through social networking features, it shares strategies between various traders. This means that you can use the app to copy someone else's trading techniques if they have been successful.

As the app is connected to a cloud platform, you can easily share your info and details between multiple devices. Meaning that if you lose your mobile device, you can always download the app on another phone and get your data back.

Forex Time FXTM

What does Forex Time FXTM have in its favor that most other platforms do not? It has a degree of trustworthiness. After all, it has been used in nearly 180 countries and regulated in numerous regions as well. The platform is designed to work for both beginners, as the app itself is fairly easy to use, and for professionals, as it gives access to advanced features and educational materials. It also offers speedy functionalities and is able to make trades with just a percentage of a second difference between the time you execute and the time the order has been confirmed.

Trade Interceptor

Trade Interceptor is mainly made for advanced users. Though it does have a friendly interface and numerous educational materials to use, it is targeted to those who have more experience dealing with the Forex market. Its main charm is the fact that it provides access to a myriad of indicators that you can use for your trades. The app is also powered by the cloud network, allowing you to transfer your profile to any device. You can even play around with a trading simulator, designed to try out your strategies before you get down to working on real trades.

TD Ameritrade

TD Ameritrade makes a comeback! Earlier, we talked about the desktop version of the app. Here, we are going to focus on the mobile version. Not only is the app one of the most established and trusted platforms in the U.S., but it is also regulated (as we have seen before). The information on the app is presented in a clear manner. TD Ameritrade also focuses on other products such as futures, stocks, and options.

Chapter 10: STOP LOSS

Always make sure that you have your stop losses in place when you begin to trade. These will ensure that you keep your losses to a minimum and help you to keep any of your profits as well. These stop points tell the market when you want to exit, even if you are asleep and can't watch your computer all the time. The stop losses can do a great job of keeping you in the game, limiting your losses, and preventing more risk than is necessary.

First, you must step a stop loss for losing money. This needs to be placed at the point where you are comfortable losing that much money. When the market goes down and reaches that point, your trade will be closed, and you will just have to settle that loss. Even if the market continues to go down, your stop loss took you out and ensured you didn't lose more money.

If you had gotten into the market without the stop loss, you might have wanted to stay in the market and hoped that things got better. Or the downturn may have happened while you were asleep, and you wouldn't be able to fix the issue. Either way, this stop loss can help save you a bunch of money.

You should also put in a stop loss for your profits as well. This will be at the place where you are most comfortable with the profits that you make. Doing this ensures that if the stock reaches that certain point, you will be able to walk away with a profit. This way, if you are away from the computer for some reason, and the currency hits your profit point, but then takes a sharp turn down, you get to take the profit because the system took you out before the downturn occurred. This helps you to maintain your profits and can do wonders for keeping your emotions out of the game.

Chapter 11: TAKE PROFIT

You don't need to be a financial expert or genius to realize that the most prominent market attraction feature is the profit potential. First, let's make it clear that the Forex market is not a platform for millionaires alone. This platform also gives a chance to traders with little capital. There are specific forex brokers who allow one to trade with as little as $25.

What then is the chance of making a profit if one can start with this low investment? One thing that you should know is that you can use leverage to trade. When you trade with leverage, you can open positions worth $10,000 while you invest as little as $25.

Another important fact about the Forex market is that any movement causes the prices to change. In other words, traders have a chance to trade to make profit or loss.

While Forex trading can be highly profitable, it is also dangerous. Therefore, you should be aware of the risk, and don't make a mistake to risk money that you can't afford to lose.

Trade opportunities
There are two trade opportunities in the Forex market.

Buy trade
The opportunity to buy trade is explained using the following scenario. Let's say that you think the current EURO value is growing strong against the US dollar, and you can opt to open a trade position to buy euros hoping that the currency value continues to be strong against the US dollar. In this case, the bearish currency is the US dollar while the bullish one is the euro.

Sell trade
On the other hand, if you have a strong belief that the euro should weaken against the US dollar, you may choose to open a trade position to sell Euros hoping that the value of the currency decreases. In the following scenario, the US dollar is bullish while the Euro is bearish.

Tip

The base currency is the only place where you have a choice whether to sell or buy. The quote currency is where the opposite is applied. Therefore, if you decide to buy the EUR/USD, you'll be selling US dollars and buying Euros. When you sell the EUR/USD, you'll be buying US dollars and selling the Euro.

If you are traveling to a foreign country and you decide to exchange currency, technically, you'll be buying the currency of the nation you are visiting and selling your currency.

Even when you think you are new to Forex, you must have traded Forex before, but you didn't realize it. For instance, if you travel to another country carrying your nation's currency, you are required to have your nation's currency to be exchanged to the currency of the country you are visiting. During the exchange, you will notice that the value of the two currencies is not equal. The value may be less or more.

Currency exchange is not only for travelers. Even the difference in price can be a motivation for you to trade. Across the world, thousands of financial transactions happen every hour. Many of these transactions involve organizations exchanging the value of one currency for another. With so many currency exchange rates taking place, the currency values are dynamic.

When compared to another, the value of one currency may be higher during the day because of economic and political news. This means that in the evening, currency may be weaker than another but then become stronger by midnight. These dynamic changes in the currency value are what cause Forex traders to make profit or loss in the Forex markets.

Forex is commonly known as foreign exchange or FX, and it involves the buying and selling of different currencies with the aim of making profits based on the changes in the value. The forex market is the largest market in the world; it is larger than the stock exchange market. Therefore, it attracts many traders. There is high liquidity in the foreign exchange market, and as such, this attracts both the experienced and the beginner traders. In fact, the forex trade market is so large that all the stock markets in the world cannot match its capacity. The foreign exchange market is decentralized across the globe; therefore, all the different currencies in the world are traded freely.

The Forex Market

Currently, the forex market has an approximated USD 5 trillion traded each day, and as such, the liquidity outdoes every other market across the world. This indicates that anyone can purchase almost all the currencies he/she wants in the volumes he/she wants so long as the market is open. The forex market is usually open 24 hours every day for 5 days a week starting from Monday to Friday. The trade begins with the opening of the Australia market, then Asia, Europe and finally The United States of America until the close. During summer, the forex market opens on Sunday at 9.00 pm Greenwich meridian time and closes on Friday at 9.00 pm GWM. However, during winter the market operates between 10.00 pm and 10.00 pm accordingly. The trading hours ensure that the currencies are traded at all hours of the day and night. While some other trade instruments can become untradeable due to downfalls of their markets, the forex trade can always find a seller and a buyer regardless of the state of the market.

Chapter 12: CANDLESTICKS

The majority of beginner traders are advised to look for particular candlestick formations that align with resistance and support. This style dictates that one has to be very careful and selective about the trade he/she picks and to stick to the sidelines until everything looks perfect. This style has a chance of making profits, but many people find it hard to make more than just a small margin of profit. There are a number of reasons why people do not make a lot of profit with this style. First, it is very hard to find a set up that looks perfect; therefore, the traders will let many opportunities go. Secondly, the style has very difficult effects on the psychology of the trader because he/she has to sit on the side and watch an otherwise good move get lost.

Consequently, the trader might get itchy fingers in the trade and dive in too deep. Thirdly, when used on its own, candlestick analysis is almost useless. It is used in combination with resistance, support, time of the day, trend and other factors.

All the mentioned factors are more powerful in themselves than the candlesticks, and yet the trader is taught to focus on the candlestick before any other thing. Another weakness of the Candlestick analysis is that it ignores quantitative and fundamental factors.

One of the strongest indicators that the market is ranging is when a tweezer bottom candlestick pattern emerges. If this happens at the same time as a Fibonacci retracement, resistance and support level or relevant pivot level, then you will know the signal is almost too strong to contain. If this is the case, then you will be able to make a profit from trading at this level rather than waiting for the confirmation of a ranging price based on the way it reacts to the opposite band as you normally would.

This pattern is also easy to spot as it is actually made up of two different, separate, forex candle patterns. The first candle, known as the setup candle, is either going to be notably bullish or bearish and will ideally occur at the tail end of a substantial price push down. This candle represents the last vestiges of the downwards price surge and also a failure back from the low price.

The second candle is known as the confirmation candle and is always going to be bullish. The confirmation candle will have a peak price or lower wick that will match quite closely, or even exactly, with that of the setup candle. The stronger the signal, the greater the length of the confirmation candle wick. This represents the amount of low point rejection that is taking place.

Fundamentals to keep in mind: The tweezer bottom candlestick pattern is going to most commonly occur at the end of a trend towards decreasing prices, regardless if this is part of a larger trend or simply a short overall retracement. If this takes place at the end of a long-running price decrease, then it likely indicates that the supply of sellers is just about to run dry.

This then naturally means that the market of buyers who are eager for opportunities is going to be primed for action and more likely to jump into the market as the levels of the currency pair in question appear quite cheap. If there is a bear and bull struggle taking place as well, keep in mind that it is likely the bulls will come out on top. After this happens, the price will often settle near the higher point on the confirmation candle as well as at a point that is above where it started.

The tweezer bottom is also more likely to occur during a positive trend that causes the price to retrace to that of a previous support level. This will also cause some downward movement in part due to buyers striving to make a profit while at the same time sellers who are slow to move into the market in part thanks to inflated prices and in part simply because it is easy to see the overall number of buyers drying up. This, in turn, often causes the price to decrease to a level when buyers will once again be interested. This, eventually, will cause the price to be pushed up once again.

Generally speaking, in order to maximize the value potential from this situation, you are going to want to purchase a buy stop at a point between two and five pips above the highest price the confirmation candle has reached so far. If you are extremely confident about the state of the market, you could also choose to place an order that is at market. Regardless of your choice, you are still going to want to place a stop that is anywhere between two and five pips below the bottom most point of the tweezer bottom candlestick.

As always, this advice is simply a general guide as the current level of market volatility is going to play a huge part in where you place your stops. If you are working with a longer timeframe then setting a stop that is up to 20 pips below or above the current price is a perfectly viable strategy. The greater the size of the bullish confirmation candle, the greater the likelihood that the price is going to increase. This is only true up to a point, however, as if it is too long then you might have a difficult time finding an adequate risk and reward ratio.

As an example, if you set a stop loss that is 50 pips below the tweezer bottom just to manage the trade correctly and you know that there is resistance at 20 pips above the current price action then you can consider the trade to have a low possibility of success and pass on it.

Engulfing candlestick

In order to confirm the signals that you find in the bouncing Bollinger band strategy, you will want to be on the lookout for either bearish or bullish engulfing candlestick patterns. You can also look for an evening star. This type of candlestick pattern is made up of a pair of forex candles, both the confirmation and the signal are going to be contained within the second candle which is known as the confirmation candle. You will be able to recognize it due to its large body that completely consumes the setup candle. At close, the confirmation candle will have a lower overall price than the setup candle.

This type of pattern often starts near the top before continuing upward regardless of whether that move is connected to a retracement or a longer trend. If it appears at the end of the protracted price increase, then this is a signal that the supply of buyers is filling out the seller's market. Assuming this occurs, more sellers than ever are likely to jump on the bandwagon thanks to the high price of the currency pair. With one focused move, they then defeat the buyers by exceeding the bullish effort found in previous candles and reversing the price in the process.

You can also find a similar pattern in a downward trend assuming the price temporarily retraces to a predetermined resistance level. This typically occurs when a variety of different sellers all take their profits at once and buyers move in to rapidly take advantage of the deflating pricing. This can also occur as part of a normal period of market exhaustion. This, in turn, causes the price to move upward to a level where sellers can once again be reasonably interested in the currency and start pushing the price in a downward direction once more.

Bullish engulfing pattern: The bullish engulfing pattern is also made up of two separate candles, with both the confirmation and signal found within the second candle. In this pattern, the setup candle is bearish and typically occurs after a hard-downward price push. The second candle is also going to be bullish and contains a body that essentially engulfs the setup candle. The closing price of this candle is also greater than the setup candle.

The bullish engulfing pattern tends to set itself up at the bottom point of a downward price trend and typically signals that sellers are in low supply and the market is starting to favor buyers. This will attract new buyers who like the cheap price. In a concentrated push, they then overpower the sellers and exceed the bearish leaning, reversing the direction of the price.

Assuming this scenario forms during an uptrend, the price will naturally retrace itself to a support point and the downward move will cause additional sellers to take advantage of the high prices. This, in turn, will also cause the price to gently move in that same downward direction until the buyers are once again willing to bite. When this occurs, the price will move upward once more.

Chapter 13: FOREX QUOTE BASICS

Forex (Foreign Exchange Market) is the biggest financial market in the world. Therefore, Forex trading refers to Currency exchange trading As you know, it is extremely important for currencies to exist in this world.. Without them, people will not be able to buy and sell goods. Now, these goods will not always be bought and sold in the local country alone and will also have to be bought from a foreign country. Now say for example your line in Germany and wish to buy a laptop from China. The German currency is Euro, and Chinese currency is Yuan. Now, when you wish to buy the laptop, the Chinese seller will most likely not accept the Euro as payment, but would accept Dollars, as up until now, Dollars is the most widely accepted currency and easy to convert into Yuan as he will want the Yuan, which is the ultimately currency he will want in his bank account in China. So, you will have to exchange your Euro for Dollars to pay the Chinese seller. Here, you have to understand that the currency will get converted to certain "Exchange rate" quoted by the market at the time the conversion occurs. This "rate" will always be a difference in the values of the currencies. This difference will always prove to be an advantage for one country and a disadvantage to another in ways that we could analyze in the future.

Now say 1 Euro is valued at 20 Yuan. This means that the German trader can exchange 1 Euro for 20 Yuan and 100 Euro for 2000 Yuan. Here, the Yuan trails the Euro, which means that Germany is in a better place in terms of forex trading. On the other hand, if a trader in China were to buy wine from Germany then he would have to pay a lot more towards it due to the difference in rates between the two currencies. This is just an example, and the difference in rates can be quite different from this. It can be higher or lower in value.

Now here, a buyer wanted to exchange the money because they wished to buy something from a foreign seller, but Forex is not always traded for this reason alone. It is also traded to capitalize upon the difference in values. You could be able to make big profits if you play the game right, but there are certain things that you must learn about first in order to invest in the Forex market.

CONCEPTS OF FOREX TRADING

The majors

The very first concept that you must understand is the majors. The majors refer to the major currencies that are regularly traded in the Forex market. The stock market has thousands of shares that the trader can choose from to invest in. This more often than not ends up confusing the trader and might also cause them to make the wrong investments. But this problem is tackled in the Forex market, as there are certain major currencies that you can trade in on a regular basis. These are based on trends and after understanding which countries provide you with the best overvalued and undervalued advantages. Here is the list of the 8 major countries that you can turn to in order remain with the highest profit.

The United States of America

Canada

Europe

United Kingdom

Switzerland

Australia

New Zealand

Japan

These countries and their currencies are identified as the big 8 because they have the best financial markets and/or manufacturing capabilities. These facts allow their currencies to always remain in demand for exchange. If you exchange any of these currencies in the right moment, your investment will surely be safe. For that, you have to constantly follow the economic scene of all the individual countries.

Buy and sell

You have to understand that the Forex market works in a simultaneous buying and selling fashion. This means that if you want to buy one currency, you will have to sell the one you have at the same time. This is easy to understand if you have, for example, physical Euros, and walk into a Bank and exchange for physical Dollars. You sell your Euros and purchased Dollars. One transaction that includes buy and sell.

But in the Forex world, we trade Forex symbols called "pairs." So, when you are buying one currency, you will automatically be selling another. In the simple example mentioned above, you traded the pair EUR/USD. In a trading platform, you use this symbol if you want to buy Euros (in Dollars) or Dollars (in Euros). All pairs or symbols have the same principle. If you "buy the symbol" you are buying the first currency if you "sell the symbol" you are buying the second currency. You have to get used to this concept in order to trade in Forex. You will have to calculate the basis points of the currencies based on their difference. That you can calculate by looking at the trending rates of the two currencies. The basis points refer to a measure of the interest or any percentages that you need to calculate before you go ahead with a deal. You will be able to calculate your gain by doing so.

Rate of return

The rate of return in the forex market is quite large. This means that you can remain with a big profit or a big loss depending on your investment. There have been cases of people making millions by just investing a few hundred or thousand dollars. This is possible if you know to invest in the market the right way. Let's say you invest $10 in the market and it gives you a return of $1000. That is highly possible in the currency market. However, if you get it wrong, then you might end up losing a lot of money. The currency market is extremely volatile, and you have to remain abreast of the difference in values of the currencies. The idea is to look for currencies that are momentarily undervalued, that way, you can expect a big change in value to finally close the transaction at your desired profit. The prices of the currencies are going to cause you a loss, then you must sell them off.

Dual benefits

The forex market offers you dual benefits when you invest in the market. It is better known as the Currency Carry Trade. The Currency Carry Trade is one where the person stands to benefit in two ways. Let us look at an example. Now let's say a Chinese trader exchanges 5000 Yuan for dollars and buys a bond with the dollars' worth. The trader will receive an interest of 5% on the bond provided the rate of exchange between the two countries remains the same. If it does, then the trader will stand to gain a profit of 50% owing to the difference in the currency values. This is an added benefit to the fact that the trader will also be able to avail a profit from selling the bond later. Here, you have to understand that the exchange rate between the two should remain the same otherwise the trader will lose money. This risk is quite high with currencies whose rates are quite volatile. You will not be able to predict the difference in rates, and by the time you withdraw from it, you probably would have lost quite some money. The difference in the rates usually occurs over a period of years and will not be within a short period of time.

OTC

Unlike the regular Stock Market (that deals with regulated Financial Instruments), Forex is always traded OTC (over the counter). This means that the currencies are not considered "financial instruments" in most countries and are not regulated as such. Banks and Brokers trade currencies via an Electronic Communication Network (ECN). A medium that is different from a stock market exchange like NYSE or AMEX. A dealer will be responsible for the trade, and there will be no centralized control over the trade. It is the same manner in which penny stocks and bonds are exchanged. You will have to do some homework on how you can start trading in your local market as the method differs from country to country. You have to look at dealers that will help you get these currencies. All Banks and Brokers, authorized to exchange, are connected to this network. In essence, you need an authorized bank or broker to handle your orders via the internet. These form the different basic concepts of forex that you have to understand if you wish to trade in it. They will act as your guide when you partake in forex trading.

Chapter 14: TRADING PLATFORMS

For centuries now, traders have used Forex Tools to increase productivity through improved performance. Ever since the early times of human existence, people have evolved and learned how to use tools to make their life easier. Imagine that some years back, people would not easily communicate with each other and currently, people are communicating with each other as soon as they want regardless of the time and the distance.

Tools are literally indispensable in life especially in the current years, and this case also applies for forex trading too. Brokers make a point of providing traders with some of the most advanced trading platforms to help them get the best experience and maximize profits. One example of this is Meta4, but many tools are more powerful and other features that enhance the trading experience. Without trading tools, Foreign exchange can be very challenging for both the new and seasoned traders. As such, many traders look to complement their decision-making skills through the use of different trading tools. The tools help the trader determine the most profitable exit and entry point.

Forex tools are provided by the brokers and platform providers for free, or the user may be required to subscribe for some. Some of the free tools offered by most websites dealing with forex and financial news are the economic calendars. Some forex signal trading services also provide the traders with trading cues that help the beginner traders.

Some popular online trading platforms such as Meta Trader 4 offer a compilation of the best trading tools. In particular, Meta Trader 4 offers a cover –all package of trade indicators and trade automation options.

Fundamental analysis tools are some of the popular and most useful tools of the trade that a trader can get online for free. Some of these tools include the economic news calendar and financial newswire access. Other tools of trade available for the trader can be found on different platforms and forex news.

Economic News Calendar Tool

Economic news calendar is one of the most essential and useful tools of the trade used by traders. The list informs the trader of the future market consensus and also the previously released information about the relevant geopolitical events and key economic data. The calendar also lays out the timings of monetary policymakers' speeches, central bank policy statement, and elections. Fundamental analysts have a special interest in the calendar because of the fundamental economic releases that will affect a country's currency. The typical providers of these calendars include brokers and news websites.

Financial Newswire Access

As a supplement to the calendar, economic news gets disseminated by a range of financial publications. The news outlets include respected newspapers and financial wires such as Reuters, Market Watch, Journal, and the Financial Times. There are also other publications and source online that are less know but viable. These tools analyze the important economic news, geopolitical and geographical events, and other resources such as gold and oil that can affect the urgencies value.

Pip Calculator

A typical pip calculator may also show the value of a pip for a particular pair based on a mini lot, micro lot, or standard lot. To use the calculator, one simply needs to enter the position details that include the currency pair, the trade size, the amount of money in the account, the position size parameters and the leverage. The calculator works out the value of the pip for each position in the chosen currency. The tool is very useful for the trader to keep track of the value of a position in the account.

The Currency Correlation Tool/Correlation Matrix

The forex market is made up of many pairs of currencies and there exists known correlations that one can easily calculate. The correlations can either be positive or negative, and they will be more pronounced in some currency pairs than in others. Having a negative correlation indicates that the pairs will move in different directions. A positive correlation means that the pairs will move in the same direction. A trader who seeks to diversify will normally opt for the negatively correlated pairs.

Broker Spread Comparison Tool

Many of the spread comparison sites show the spreads that are quoted by the brokers usually on major currency pairs. Majority of the spread comparison websites allow a trader to filter timeframe, session or currency pair, therefore, giving a trader an edge when selecting the broker with most affordable dealing spreads. Once the trader has selected the broker, a spread comparison tool becomes pretty useless because switching the brokers after a selection can be very costly.

Forex Time Zone Converter

The periods when a trader chooses to participate in the market can make a major difference to their gains. The major forex trading centers in the world include London, Tokyo, New York, and Sydney and they all operate in different time zones. However, to some degree, the business hours of these centers overlap with Sydney opening the market on Monday at 5 pm NY time and closing at 5 pm on Friday NY time. One of the most useful tools that a trader can have when trading is a graph that shows the times that the different centers are operating. This is true because a trader will be able to identify the moments when the markets are overlapping, and these are usually the most active and liquid times. Remember that the three most essential ingredients of trading are volatility, liquidity, and activity.

Forex Volatility Calculator

As seen earlier, one of the most essential elements of trading is market volatility. The currency pairs with limited ranges are barely the best currencies for trading. There is no difficulty in calculating the volatility, but with the numerous numbers of pairs available for trade in the market, it is better if the trader allows a properly programmed computer to handle the task. Typically, a forex volatility calculator will determine the volatility of every pair in real time by taking historical exchange rate information. Another aspect of a good forex volatility calculator is that it breaks down the volatility into different timeframes for instance weekly, monthly, quarterly and annually. This helps the trader to determine if an option is too volatile or not.

Forex Trading Platforms

Meta Trader 4 is the most used online trading platform, and so far, no other platform matches it. The platform has a variety of features that are literally indispensable for a serious trader.

This platform offers a wholesome technical analysis functionality which allows traders to map out currencies in real time. It also allows the trader to apply a variety of technical oscillators and other relevant indicators to the currencies. The platform also has a functionality that is fully integrated to allow the trader to trade currencies directly from the charts. An extra advantage of the Metatrader4 is that traders can use it to transact with most of the forex brokers online. Again, a large group of people use the platform; therefore, if one runs into problems when using it, he/she can ask for help. Meta Trader 4 also supports expert advisor software and automated trading.

Meta Trader 4 also allows the trader to add their own parameters in the premade and custom indicators. Besides the stock exchange, MT4 allows traders to deal in other asset classes such as energy products, metals, and stocks so long as they are supported by an online broker. Doubtlessly, MetaTrader4 is by far one of the best, useful and complete forex trading tools in the market and it is obtainable for free from the website of the developer. Always open a demo account and practice before investing with real money.

Keeping a Trading Journal

One might underestimate the importance of keeping a journal that records the history of different trades. An accurate journal is one of the most essential tools that helps a trader determine their next move. It is important to keep track of the details of each trade, for instance, the time a trade was initiated, why, and if it was liquidated, what the driver was. The trader will be able to assess his/her trading habits from this information, learn from mistakes, and mitigate risks in the future.

Chapter 15: TECHNICAL AND TECHNICAL INDICATORS

This particular method relies too much on the stochastic by itself and I do no recommend using this unless you have a certain level of experience in the markets. The midpoint of the indicator, that is 50, is a significant level to watch since it indicates which side of the market has greater momentum. The upper half generally signifies the bulls are exerting greater pressure and the lower half belongs to the bears. If you look back to the calculation of the indicator, you'll understand why this is. A level below 50 indicates that price is in the lower half of the look back period and a level above 50 indicates price is in the upper half of the price range in the look back period. Any time the oscillator crosses the midway point, we ought to be on the lookout for a change in conditions or some sort of a violent reaction from price.

Another type of setup to look for is when the price prints, for example, a lower high but the indicator prints a higher high. Or conversely, price prints a higher low but the indicator prints a lower low. This, while not a pure divergence, nonetheless indicates that the momentum and price characteristics don't match and that there is an entry possible in the direction of the prevalent trend. Again, the very fact that such a pattern has occurred is not enough to justify an entry. Ideally, a trader will look for confirmation using the methods previously describe to determine the most likely entry point.

This concludes our look at the Stochastic oscillator. It should be evident by now why this indicator is so popular and is considered powerful in technical analysis circles. Te variety of signals it throws up makes it slightly intimidating at first and indeed this indicator is prone to being misread by beginners, especially within the extremes where traders might confuse this as being overbought or oversold. This alone is the biggest cause of the false signals that has dogged this indicator and understanding the mechanics of the stochastic extremities will go a long way towards helping you trade successfully.

FIBONACCI

Fibonacci numbers start with 0 and 1 and then increase exponentially from there by adding the 2 previous numbers together to get the next number in the sequence. As such it starts off with 0, 1, 2, 3, 5 and so on and so forth. The difference between these numbers is known as the Fibonacci ratio which includes .236, .382, .5 and so on and so forth. Finding these ratios in the pairs you are considering allows you to determine naturally occurring entry and exit points.

Using the Fibonacci sequence to perform a retracement gives you the ability to determine how much an asset moved in price initially. It uses multiple horizontal lines to point out resistance or support at either 23.6, 38.2, 50, 61.8 or 100 percent. When used properly they make it easier to identify the spots transactions should be started, what prices to target and what stop losses to set.

This doesn't mean that you should apply the Fibonacci retracements blindly as doing so can lead to failure as easily as it can success. It is important to avoid choosing inconsistent reference points which can easily lead to mistakes as well as misanalysis, for example, mistaking the wick for the body of a candle. Retracements using the Fibonacci sequence should always be applied wick-to-wick which in turn leads to a clearly defined and actionable resistance level.

Likewise, it is important to always keep the big picture in mind and keep an eye on trends that are of the longer variety as well. Failing to keep the broad perspective in mind makes short-term trades more likely to fail as it makes it harder to project the correct momentum and direction any potential opportunities might be moving in. Keeping the larger trends in mind will help you pick more reliable trades while also preventing you from accidentally trading against a specific trend.

Don't forget, Fibonacci retracements are likely to indicate quality trades, but they will never be able to do so in a complete vacuum. It is best to start with a retracement and then apply other tools including stochastic oscillators or MACD. Moving ahead without confirmation will leave you with little except positive thoughts and wishes that the outcome goes the way you want. Remember, there is no one indicator that is strong enough to warrant moving forward on a trade without double checking the validity of the data.

The other limitation of a Fibonacci retracement is that it doesn't work reliably over shorter time frames as there is simply too much interference from standard market volatility which will result in false apparent levels of support as well as resistance. What's more, the addition of whipsaws and spikes can make it difficult to utilize stops effectively which can result in tight and narrow confluences.

While a singular Fibonacci retracement can be meaningful on its own from time to time, two or more Fibonacci retracements or extensions that show the same thing are almost always going to lead to viable results. The concept of overlapping Fibonacci retracements is one that most traders discover on their own over time. It commonly includes the use of other types of retracements or extensions with the purpose of determining a variety of signals including support and resistance levels as well as relevant pivot points.

As such, a group of overlapping retracements is a significant improvement as two strong Fibonacci levels are all that are required in order to determine a reliable trade in many cases. Specifically, the presence of a pair of Fibonacci levels at a point of known resistance or support is almost always enough to yield viable results. The simplicity of this strategy is one of its greatest strengths and many traders use it to the exclusion of all else when trading in the forex market.

Using this strategy: When it comes to utilizing this strategy correctly, you can use any chart that you like as long as it contains either a run down or a run up of a given currency price in addition to multiple retracements. From there, you will need to begin adding Fibonacci lines to the chart. If you draw these Fibonacci lines on a powerful down trend, then you will be able to start from the high point on the chart before moving toward the lowest swing point. If you are following an uptrend, then the reverse is going to be true. Once this is done you will need to find the confluence points that comes from any Fibonacci level including 38 percent, 50 percent, 62 percent and 79 percent.

Fibonacci extensions: To use Fibonacci extensions with this strategy, the basics are going to be more or less the same. You are simply going to choose the chart of your choice before adding in the Fibonacci lines with the Fibonacci extensions enabled as well. A particularly useful time to utilize this strategy is when the market is ranging between the support and resistance levels. It doesn't matter if the actual range is long or short, it will eventually break because the market cannot stay in an indecisive position forever.

At this point, you will need to wait for the price to break past the lowest support line as if this does not occur then you are going to want to close out your position and try your luck again the next time the price starts following the trade in question. If the price does ultimately break through the lower support line, then you are going to wait for it to retest the broken support so that you can confidently close out your position before waiting for the price to once more come into alignment with the trend. Once it breaks past the support line but fails to crest above it, then you are going to want to take the relevant position based on the trend and set a level of 161.80 as the new target.

Assuming the trend breaks at this point and presents itself in such a way that it appears as though it is strong enough to continue to 423.60 then you will want to ensure you have the proper position and set this as your target while putting the stop loss slightly above 261.80.

Mistakes to avoid

While Fibonacci levels can provide a great deal of insight into the trading process, it can also lead to serious issues and massive losses if used incorrectly. As such, you are going to want to be aware of the following commonly made mistake sin order to ensure that your strategy works out according to plan.

Avoid mixing reference points: In order to correctly fit your retracements to the relevant price action, you are always going to want to keep steady reference points. This means that if you are using a low trend as a reference past the close of a session or in the body of a candle, then your ideal high price should always be visible in the candle at the top of the trend. Mistake and misanalysis can make it easy to accidentally skew these reference points by moving from the wick to the body of the candle hurting your potential for profit in the process. Luckily, consistently holding on to your reference points will also make it easier for you to determine accurate support and resistance levels at the moment.

Avoid ignoring long-term trends: If you get in the habit of dealing with short term charts then it can be easy to lose focus on the big picture. This narrowing of your perspective can ultimately result in misguided short-term trades if you aren't careful. Keeping a close eye on long-term trends, even if you don't plan on actively trading them can help you determine if the short-term trends you have found are all that they appear cracked up to be. Even better, this level of perception will allow you to potentially act on trends that have a great deal of momentum turning a solid 50 pip profit into one that is 400 pips or more.

MOVING AVERAGE

Moving averages refer to using the power of the trend to assess the direction of the market. As you know, it is extremely important for you to be able to predict how the value of the currency will move next. For this, it is best to go through the different trends that the value of the currency has been following in the recent past. The basic idea is to trace the trend that the price has been following. How is it moving ahead, where does the price reversal point lie, at what point is it most profitable to sell the currency, etc.?

BOLLINGER BANDS

The Bollinger band strategy is defined as the continuation trading strategy that uses the technical indicator called 20-period moving average to identify the trend direction. These bands are good for measuring the volatility of the instrument one is trading, and it is used to form a basis of swing trading in the forex market.

The Bollinger bands indicator consists of three lines; lower band, top band, and middle band. When a trader or an analyst is using the Bollinger band settings for the strategy, the three lines represent;

- **The Top Line** - two standard deviations from the moving average to the upper side
- **The Middle Line -** is the moving average for 20 periods
- **The Lower Line** - two standard deviations from the moving average to the downside (middle line)

A trader may try to change the band setting in search or the perfect settings, but there is hardly any such thing. Therefore, anyone who tells you that they are selling the best settings is being dishonest.

The theory behind the Bollinger band is that the two bands (upper and lower) contain price action. This means that any price movements touching or exceeding the upper or lower band indicates increased volatility within the market.

The Trading Rules of Bollinger Bands

Trading the support and resistance of the band lines

A trader can use the upper and lower bands as support and resistance indicators whereby; if the price touches the lower and upper bands and reverses, that indicates the probability of a major move.

Trading the fixed horizontal lines combined with the band lines

In this method, the trader looks for the horizontal resistance and support levels which coincide with the prices that are touching the lower and upper band. The trader should ensure that the price has reversed on this support or resistance level at least once. This makes that trade signal reliable.

Trading the breakout

While trading the breakouts, a trader should watch for the trend process as they break through the lower and upper Bollinger bands. The trader should also ensure that the candlestick is closed above the upper line before entering and that it closes below the lower line before exiting. This technique works best on a trending market.

Trading the squeeze

Firstly, the price must be pushing between the lower and upper bands. Under such circumstances, the market has low volatility. The trader should wait for the breakouts which can either be upwards or downwards. The Bollinger band helps a trader to identify the push and capitalize on the breakout happening afterward. One can place a pending stop order on the two sides' right outside the squeeze. These stop orders will be triggered once the break out happens. When one stop order is activated, the trader may cancel the other one. The trader should then place a stop loss order halfway through the squeeze or on the other side.

Another style of trading with Bollinger band squeeze that a trader can use is to wait for the breakout, once it happens, wait for the price to reverse till it touches the middle band, and then enter the order.

STOCHASTICS

The Stochastic oscillator is a popular technical analysis tool and with good reason. Developed in the 1950's by George Lane, this indicator provides great insight in to the existing momentum of an instrument. Its popularity arises from the fact that the indicator doesn't follow the closing price or indeed any other parameter which one might first think of while looking at a chart. It purely measures momentum. Since momentum has a tendency to slow down prior to a reversal, the Stochastic oscillator sometimes serves as a leading indicator to price despite being a trailing indicator of momentum.

Visually, this indicator consists of 2 lines which cross over each other and 2 extreme levels at the top and bottom of the indicator window. The values fluctuate between 0 to 100 and the indicator compares what the current price looks like compared to the highest and lowest price within the look back period. Traders can change this setting from the default value of 14. The exact number is something which, as mentioned previously, depends on every individual. There is a danger of turning this into a holy grail quest so resist that temptation. A good rule of thumb is to see how closely the stochastic curve follows price. There will be times when the stochastic will print a divergence from price and this is normal, because this indicator measures momentum which fluctuates depending on the trend. The best method would be to tailor the look back period based on the volatility of the given instrument. Another optimizer for the oscillator is to use it with another trend measuring indicator, like the ones we've looked at previously.

This indicator is not infallible of course. It is indeed notorious for giving false signals especially in strong trends. This stands to reason since momentum ebbs and flows as price moves and a strong trend can reach the extreme levels of the indicator pretty quickly and stay there as the trend continues. There are ways to avoid this but for now it bears to keep in mind that this indicator needs to be used with another trend indicator to increase its relevance.

The main difference between the 2 versions is that the slow stochastic is less choppy and produces lesser cross overs between the lines. Some traders prefer it because of this but you do have to keep in mind some signals will naturally be filtered out. The key is not to achieve 100% accuracy but to reach a stage where the indicator gives us a good approximation of the market. There is a third version of the oscillator called the full version but in my opinion this only adds more confusion and is an attempt to find a magic key to unlock market secrets. As such, I will not be covering this version. The interpretation of all the versions is the same though. The upper section and lower section, usually 80 and 20 respectively, indicate high momentum levels is their direction respectively.

So when a security is trending and we see the stochastic oscillator printing a value greater then 80, we can conclude that the instrument is trading near the highs of its look back period. This does not mean that such a reading is bearish. Similarly, neither does an reading below 20 indicate that a bullish reversal is on the cards. Misunderstanding this point is what causes most traders to lose money and thus blame the indicator for providing false signals. The key to avoiding this is to filter for the trend currently and to look for the opposite signal. In plain English, it means we look for the occasional signal <20 in an uptrend and >80 signal in a downtrend. The logic behind this is we want to ride the trend till it ends. Therefore a signal <20 in an uptrend indicates, price is about to jump higher so we use that as a signal to jump on board.

Another entry method to look for with the stochastic oscillator is when divergences form. A divergence is when the oscillator does not print the same pattern as price does, for example, is price makes a new low but if the indicator makes a higher low, this should be considered a bullish signal. Similarly a bearish divergence is when price prints a higher high but the indicator shows a lower high. The divergence itself should not be the entry point and traders ought to wait for some form of confirmation of trend reversal before entering. Such a confirmation can be in the form of a price pattern or another indicator like a moving average crossing over etc. Another method, though slightly more complicated, involves using support and resistance along with the stochastic level itself. A bullish divergence can be confirmed when price breaks above a resistance point and the indicator crosses above 50. Similarly, a bearish divergence can be confirmed when price breaks a support level and the indicator dips below 50.

There are inherent flaws in this way of confirmation, most of all to do with the fact that the best confirmations come from another indicator derived from another aspect of price behavior.

The charts on the following pages illustrate how this indicator is used.

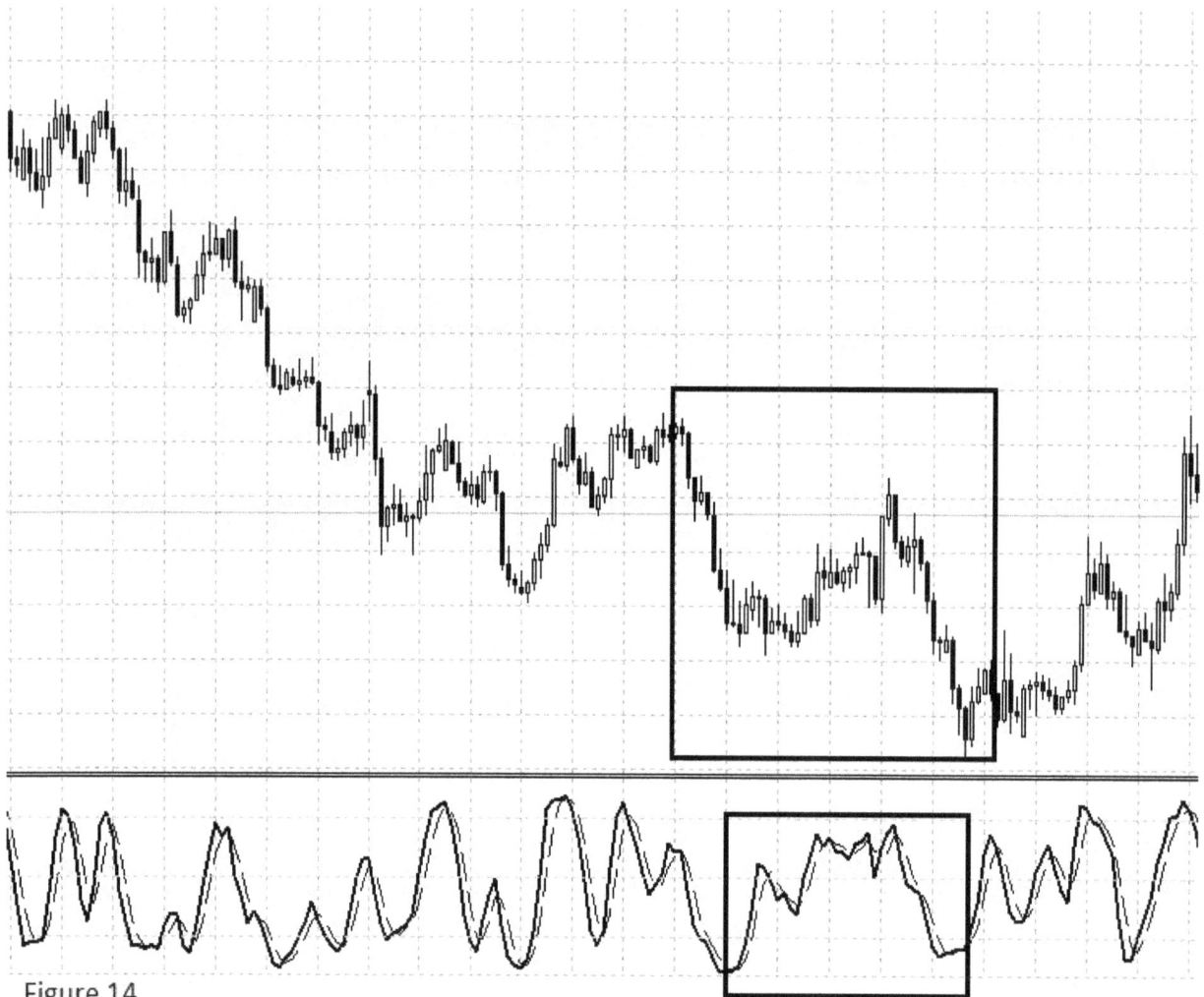

Figure 14

Figure 14 shows a textbook example of a bullish divergence. Here we see price making new lows but the stochastic prints a higher low. Also, to the left, notice how the oscillator ought to be used to take advantage of the existing bear trend. The indicator routinely goes up into the extreme level, that is, greater than 80, on pullbacks into the trend. This ought to put us on alert that the pullback is ending but by itself it doesn't constitute an entry signal. This is a mistake most traders make and is one you ought to avoid. Used in conjunction with another indicator, entry signals become a lot clearer.

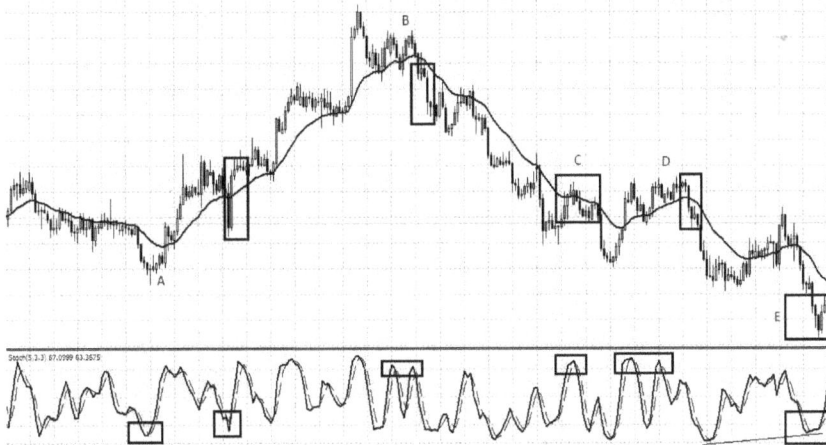

Figure 15

Figure 15 gives us a great look at the number of ways this indicator helps us determine the course of price. Here we have price that started reversed into an uptrend, stalled and then went back all the way down. A walkthrough this chart will help illustrate how the stochastic helps us predict turnaround in advance. The 20 EMA is also plotted along with price so we can explore how this indicator can be used with a traditional trend indicator. I highly recommend printing out this chart separately and covering it with another piece of paper and reading the text side by side while slowly uncovering it. Once you've read through the walkthrough, do it by yourself and see which points I have missed (on purpose) and try to interpret the price action.

We start at the left of the chart where price has been in a downtrend (not shown) and at point A, makes a new low. Price is still firmly below the 20 EMA so we have no reason to suspect anything but the stochastic tells us a different story. While price is forming new lows, the indicator is near he previous low. This is a major divergence from the price chart and our interest on the bullish side ought to be piqued. This is, however, not an entry indicator by itself so we wait. The most logical thing to do would be to wait for price to break to the upside of the 20 EMA. This does happen soon after and we can enter on the bar that closes above the EMA with a stop below it. Please note, this would be an aggressive trade entry. Executing such an entry is mentally taxing and it requires a lot of practice and experience to execute repeatedly. A more conventional practice is to wait to see how the first pullback or higher low plays out and read the signs via the indicator.

The first pullback (denoted by the rectangle after A) is a very aggressive one but is immediately repelled by the bulls. We simultaneously notice how the stochastic dipped below 20 and shot up along with price. This confirms our original thoughts about the trend being bullish and we can enter on the close of the big bullish bar with a stop below the 20 EMA or the bar right after it. Notice how price subsequently stays above the 20 EMA and seems to overextend itself. We don't exit as yet but we ought to be on the lookout for an exit sign. Our original trade is nicely in profit by now. A trailing stop below the higher lows or the EMA is the best option here. At point B, we have the first instance of a lower high being formed, or in other words, a higher high is not formed after a pullback for the first time. A glance at the indicator shows it is hovering in the extreme level above 80. Price then for the first time closes below the 20 EMA. Aggressive traders can play the short side here and conservative traders can wait to see if a lower low is formed.

Price bounces off the EMA soon enough and we can now conclude we're bearish on the market and actively looking to enter short. We can enter on a pullback to the EMA and ride the trend downwards. At points C and D we see how the stochastic can be used as a trend continuation indicator. The bullish pullback is strong but price lacks any significant follow through. Also the indicator is not showing any confirmation signs and is indeed diverging here as it prints higher peaks but price is trending downwards. This tells us that the bullish strength, while increasing, isn't reversing the trend and we ought to enter short on a break of the EMA. An aggressive push down shows bearish strength but the bullish pressure increases.

Price does make a new low at point E but the oscillator again shows us a divergence. It prints a higher low but price is making new lows. This is a similar situation at the one at point A and at the end of this chart we ought to be on the lookout for a bullish entry. I would like to point out here that a lot of the conclusions we draw depends on the prevalent trend. Price being above, below or crossing over the EMA informs a lot of our deductions about the oscillator value. This goes back to what I said previously about using this in conjunction with a trend indicator of some sort and why blindly following the oscillator in a formulaic way is a bad idea.

The Stochastic is not the only oscillator which works well with trend indicators. We will next look at the RSI or Relative Strength Index.

RELATIVE STRENGTH INDEX(RSI)

The relative strength index is a great statistical tool that you can use to check whether a currency is valued at the right price or over or under valued. It is important for you to check this, as you need to buy a currency that is valued at the right price. Once you apply this technique on the trend of the currency, you will find a number. If the number is 30 or under then the currency is oversold, and if it is 70 or higher then it means that it is overbought. Both of these can be a bad thing for any currency. So you have to steer clear off of them and look for pairs that lie in between. The calculation of RSI is generally seen as a tedious task. But the good news is that there are many software available that will easily and quickly calculate the amount for you without having to put in too much effort towards.

Chapter 16: FUNDAMENTAL ANALYSIS

In the foreign exchange, Fundamental analysis refers to the act of trading in the market based on the analysis of the global aspects that determine the demand and supply of currencies. A sizeable number of traders use both the fundamental and the technical analysis together to determent the when and where to trade. However, the traders tend to favor one over the other based on their individual investment plans and goals. To be precise, fundamental analysis studies aspects such as political forces, economic forces, and socials forces that may affect the asset. Many traders find ease in predicting the movement of prices while using supply and demand as an indicator. In simpler terms, the trader using fundamental analysis has to identify the economies that are blossoming and those that are stuck. As such, the trader has to know the whys and how an aspect will impact the trade, for instance, unemployment rates. The rates of unemployment affect the economy and the monetary policies implemented by the government and central banks, therefore, affecting the levels of demand and supply of the nation's currency worldwide.

Traders that use Fundamental analysis pay attention to the overall state of a nation's economy and identify factors such as interest rates GDP, international trade, manufacturing, and international trade among others. The impact of these factors on the currency affects the price of the currency on the forex trade. The bottom line of fundamental analysis in the forex trade and also other markets is that an asset can have a price that differs from its actual value. Consequently, markets may misprice, underprice or overprice an asset in the short term. Fundamental analysts claim that despite misquote of the currency, an asset will still go back to its actual price indicating its true value. Then we can say that the bottom line of traders who use fundamental analysis to gauge assets are looking for trading opportunities through analyzing the value of the asset, the current price and the possibility of change.

The main difference between fundamental analysis and technical analysis is that fundamental analysis pays attention to all other factors of affecting the trade apart from the price while the technical analysis focuses on the price only. As such, the technical analysis is very handy for short term traders such as those in day trading while the fundamental analysis is beneficial for the long-term traders such as those in the swing trading. The analysis of fundamental foreign exchange factors answers the long-term questions.

Chapter 17: VOLUME PRICE ANALYSIS

The many economies of the world are in a constant state of flux. You now know where to look to find out where in a cycle they currently are – and make trading decisions accordingly – but what do those cycles actually mean?

When boiled down to the basics, an economy is either going to be in a time of expansion or a time of recession. In the former case, there is an increase in economic activity and gross domestic product, which means more disposable income and thus spending, better employment levels and more demand.

A recession is basically the opposite and will see a drop in economic activity that has a blanket effect across internal markets for such things as housing and labor. If this gets bad enough or goes on for long enough, it becomes known as a depression.

Within those cycles you'll find inflation and deflation. Inflation refers to the prices being charged for items and services and usually rises when there is more demand than supply. Deflation, once again, is its opposite.

Gross domestic product refers to the overall value of those items and services that a single country generates over the course of one year. It's what the central banks tend to use to analyze the growth of the economy, which means it's also the best place to look to find out whether that country's economy is on the rise or on the decline.

It represents how much consumers are consuming, how much investment and government spending is going on and how much exporting is taking place.

Meanwhile, the "balance of payments" can tell you how healthy the economy is in comparison to others in the world, and it can do so fairly directly. It refers to all international activities and is considered to be in a good state when the country is accepting more payments from other countries than it is making.

The financial account will tell you how many international assets the country owns by looking at change in ownership. The country's budget deficit – the amount it must borrow above its income from taxes to meet the needs of its budget – will also indicate its internal economic health.

In general, what all these things will tell you is how risky the market is at the current moment. An economic decline is a time for safe bets, so it's usually when you'll find traders turning their attention to those safe currencies we discussed. In a time of increase, they will look more towards riskier currencies, which include the Canadian dollar, the Australian dollar, the New Zealand dollar, the British pound and the Euro.

Chapter 18: FOREX TRADING STRATEGIES

Once you know what to look for in a good trade, the next thing you are going to want to master is the basic short-term and long-term strategies that are most commonly used in the forex market.

In order to get an initial idea as to what a given carry trade can net you, the first step is to figure out the difference between the interest rate of the long and short currencies. With that number in mind, you will then multiply it by the number of units that you have in your position that is connected to the interest rate you are interested in, making a special point to include leverage as well. With this number in hand, you will then simply divide by 365 to find the amount of interest that you will earn each day.

When it comes to starting a new carry trade, the best time to do so is when a central bank report is released that indicates an increase in interest rates is forthcoming. After this information is released, you will find that countless traders jump on the idea of the carry trade using the currency whose interest rate is on the rise and its companion currency with the greatest overall degree of difference. Once you understand how the market is going to react to this news, it then becomes a matter of jumping on before the rush in order to ensure that your own profits are maximized as well. Remember, the longer you wait, the greater the starting differential will be and the less you will learn by an additional widening of the gap.

Basket carry: If the indicators on a given currency pair are not as strong as you may typically prefer, then a traditional carry trade might be a bit too risky to commit to whole-heartedly. If you have some type of information that makes you want to still pursue this course of action, then you will want to use a basket carry trade instead.

To do so, you will want to purchase three different currency pairs rather than just the one you are the most interested in. Each of these pairs should have varying interest rate levels so that you are virtually guaranteed to see a profit regardless of the direction the market ultimately moves in. When using this strategy, you will generally see an average profit on one of the three pairs and a small profit on the second while letting the third expire after only losing out on the transaction fees.

A carry trade is a great way to steady return on your initial investment without having to worry about watching the related currency movement too closely. This does not mean that it is always going to be the right choice in every situation, however. For example, if a country that has historically had a high interest rate suddenly dropped it dramatically in an effort to bolster their economy then those who are using it to prop up a carry trade are going to be forced to rapidly offload it, reducing the disparity for that pair even more. The same issue can occur if the reported average annual yield drops tenuously or the variance inherent in the exchange rate increases. Finally, you will want to always be on the lookout to ensure that the central bank of either country doesn't do anything to forcibly alter the current currency trajectory.

Trading in the short-term

If you are more interested in shorter timeframes than what a carry trade can offer you, then the most important thing to remember is that you are going to want to prioritize trades that allow you to remain in control at all times, both when it comes to managing risk and sticking to the plan you come up with prior to starting. This will allow you to deal in charts that offer shorter time frames than many other forex investors. This doesn't mean that you will only want to stick to the short-term charts, however, as this will unnaturally curtail your profits in a way that will only lose you money in the long run. To get started trading in the short term, the first thing that you will need to do is to find a pair of moving averages on the hourly chart. The trading platform that you use should have an option to automatically generate what you are looking for based on a predetermined time frame that you plug in. Once you have the indicators that you are looking for you will then be able to utilize them as a type of guidepost, allowing you to see how the market is moving in a time frame that will allow you to look before you act. If the resulting short moving average is less than the greater moving average, then you are going to want to lean heavily on a long position while if the opposite is true then you will need to lean on the short position in order to profit from the transaction.

Once you have found the trend that you are comfortable working with, the next is going to be to look more closely at the entries to match the direction of the trend you are looking into. Your main goal at this time should be to pick out the momentum that you have already seen on a longer chart as it is visualized on the shorter five or 15-minute charts. When taking advantage of this type of strategy, it is important to keep in mind that the timing is not always going to be in your favor when it comes to buying in. Instead, you are going to want to wait patiently for a profitable position to come along and the most reliable way to know when it arrives is to look for what is known as an exponential moving average.

When looking for this average you are going to want to keep an eye out for the trigger known as the eight-period exponential on the five-minute chart. Once this exponential starts moving in the direction of the overall trend, you will know that the strength of the trend and the speed at which it is acted upon are only going to increase. While this strategy may take a fair amount of micromanaging, it is well worth it for several reasons, starting with the fact that if you wait for the right trigger you know that other short-term traders are creating action based on the pair you are most interested in which means you can practically guarantee reliable profits for yourself if you jump in at a smart time. This strategy is also a great choice when you are first getting started in forex trading, especially if your trading capital is rather limited. This is due to the fact that it allows savvy traders to move in on specific currency pairs early enough to get a great deal before the actual momentum picks up steam and the bullish price movement pushes the pair into prohibitively expensive territory.

This is also a useful strategy if you are looking to maximize the currencies you are looking to sell as it will provide you with the opportunity to know when a mass exodus on the currency in question is going to occur, allowing you to sell when the price is still high. It is still important to keep in mind that if a price sees a retracement in the short-term then the price is likely going to swing quickly but you will still wan tot double check what you are seeing to prevent a costly mistake.

To further maximize your profits using this strategy you are going to want to set your stop losses so that they are placed below the most recent high-water mark. That is, of course, unless you are currently heavily invested in a short position in which case you will want to set your stop losses in such a way that they are above the most recent low point of the currency to ensure that you don't suffer a loss if the trend losses strength earlier than you were expecting. This makes the short-term strategy extremely versatile as long as you are able to keep your emotions in check and set the right stops and stick with them as opposed to losing yourself in the moment in hopes of seeing things turn around. This is not to say that working in the short-term is without risk, and the opposite is actually true in most cases. The short-term charts are far more likely to change with little to no notice than the long-term charts are, simply because any change that is noticed is going to be noticed first there. This means that if you hope to make money by using this strategy then you are going to want to do everything in your power to guarantee you are free to act with only a moment's notice. The best reaction in most situations is going to be waiting for the currency to return to a point of profitability before setting a new stop loss that is slightly in the money without getting greedy.

TREND AND RANGE TRADING

The average true Range indicates the average trading range for a particular period of time. A trading range is defined as that time when a currency trades between consistent low and high prices for a certain timeframe. In a trading range, the upper trading range provides price resistance while that at the bottom typically provides the support. In the case of forex trade, the predetermined amount of time is a 14 period. When the Average true range decreases, it indicates a decrease in volatility. The vice versa is true.

Average Directional Index

The average Directional Index indicates the length of each trend based on the lows and the highs over a particular timeframe. In forex trade, the time frame is usually 14 periods. The indicator is plotted as one line below the chart, and the values range between 0 and 100. When the line is above the twenty to twenty-five levels, then that indicates that a trend is beginning no matter the direction. When the trend becomes stronger, it indicates that there is increased volatility.

WHAT IS SCALPING AND HOW YOU CAN USE IT

In the world of investment and forex trade, the term scalping denotes the process of skimming for minute profits regular by entering and exiting positions several times each day. The process involves trading currencies on the basis of real-time analysis. The main aim of scalping is to maximize profit by getting into a position and staying with it for a very short timeframe and closing it for little profit. There are very many trades placed throughout the day, and most of the traders use a system that is based on a number of signals generated from technical analysis. The chart tools are made up of multiple signals that create the decision to buy or sell when they point in a similar direction. A scalper normally looks for large numbers of trade for small profits each time.

Scalping is very similar to day trading whereby a trader opens a position and closes it before the day ends, never allowing trade to go overnight. The main difference between the day trader and the scalper is that in day trading, a trader may look to trade once or twice in a day while in scalp trading; the trader is working with multiple trades in a session and is very frenetic.

While a day trader has the options of trading on the five minutes and 30 minutes charts, A scalp trader can trade off a one-minute chart or a tick chart. Particularly, a trader using scalping tries to catch the high-velocity moments occurring around the period that news and data are released into the market, for example, the GDP and everything else that is listed in the economic agenda.

Many scalp traders look to make about five or ten pips in every trade they act on. To get good profits, they repeat the process throughout the day many times. Keeping in mind that one standard lot pip has a value of about $10, if the trader makes five pips of profit, then he has made $50 at a go. If the trader did such a trade ten times a day, then he/she will have made a profit of $500.

SCALPING TECHNIQUES

A scalp broker should be very familiar with the platform that the broker is offering. Different brokers offer different benefits; therefore, the trader should at least open a practice account and interact with the services one on one. Scalping is very fast; therefore, a platform should not have room for errors. The disadvantage of having a platform with no rooms for error is that once a button is hit, there is no turning back. This means that if a trader hits a buy button while he/she intended to hit the sell button, then he/she better hope that he/she gets luck otherwise he/she is guaranteed of a loss. Such mistakes cannot be afforded in the scalp trading practice because they will lead to losses. As such, one should do a lot of practice before placing real money on the account.

A scalper should want to trade only with the most liquid pairs in the market. The most liquid pairs are usually the major pairs, for instance, EUR/USD. Also, certain sessions might be more liquid than others depending on the pair. Remember that although the market operates 24 hours a day, there is a difference in the volumes traded depending on the time.

Normally, when the London market opens, the volumes go up because London is the main trading center for foreign exchange. This market opens at 3 AM EST. On the other hand, the New York market opens at 8 am EST and the volumes being traded increase. This cycle continues. The best time to scalp is when the two major trading centers are open because the liquidity is so high. The Tokyo and Sydney centers are also major volume drivers.

BREAKOUT TRADING

Break out trading refers to the situations where a trader looks at the range made by a particular pair during certain day hours then placing a trade on either side while hoping to get a breakout. Breakout trading is particularly good when the pair has been in a tight range because that indicates that the pair will make a big move in a short while. The goal of the trader in the breakout trading is to position him/herself strategically such that once the move occurs; he/she catches the wave. In the breakout trading method, the trader determines the range where resistance and supports have been holding strongly then setting the entry points either below or above the breakout levels. The rule of thumb in this trading is to target an equal amount of pips making up the determined range.

CARRY TRADE

If you are interested in making long-term trades in the forex market, then you are going to ultimately become very familiar with the technique known as the carry trade. This strategy involves finding a currency pair that your analysis indicates should be profitable in the near future while also having the greatest amount of disparity between their two interest rates as possible. Typically, one of the currencies that you are going to want to use for this type of strategy is going to be either the Australian dollar, the New Zealand dollar or the Japanese yen. The New Zealand dollar and the Australian dollar are known to frequently have an interest rate of as high as 4.5 while the Japanese yen is known for getting as low as 0.1.

When used correctly, a carry trade is an excellent way to add value to your portfolio as they are guaranteed to generate profit every day, based largely on interest, for each day you hold onto them. When making carry trades it is important to keep in mind that payments for interest earned during the weekend won't be paid until Wednesday which makes Thursday the most profitable day of the week to close out carry trades. The carry trade is also an excellent choice for those who don't want to spend each and every minute of every day staring at a computer screen in hopes of seeing the type of movement that will generate a reasonable amount of profit.

While it has been a part of the forex trader's toolbox for decades, the carry trade gained widespread usage in the early 00s when the AUD/JPY pair spent several months with an interest rate differential that was greater than five percent. This, coupled with the fact that leverage in excess of 200:1 was widely available meant that new investors were gaining and losing millions of dollars each week in a scenario that is surprisingly similar to the rush to buy Bitcoin in the fall of 2017.

Chapter 19: ICHIMOKU TRADING STRATEGIES

IKH or Ichimoku for short looks like an extremely complicated indicator at first glance. The average Ichimoku chart contains 5 lines which seem to go all over the place. However, on closer examination, you will find that the Ichimoku cloud is an elegant and concise indicator wrapping all sorts of market information into one chart. The name itself translates from Japanese as "one look equilibrium chart". While that translation doesn't alleviate the confusion as to what this is, it actually does describe an Ichimoku chart very well.

Briefly, the objective of the Ichimoku cloud is to give the trader an instant snapshot of the market trend, support and resistance levels, momentum of the current trend and entry and exit signals. As you can imagine that's a lot of information crammed into a few lines and thus on the surface, makes Ichimoku seem confusing. This indicator works best on Japanese stocks and Yen pairs in forex. This is mainly due to the fact that the majority of traders in Asian markets use this indicator thus making it more efficient. The "cloud" refers to all the lines within an Ichimoku chart and is comprised of the following lines:

• Kijun Sen- Also referred to as the standard line or base line. The usual setting for this line is 26. This translates, on a daily chart, as the midpoint of the high-low range over a period of 26 days. The calculation is shown below:

Base line= (26 period high+ 26 period low)/2

• Tenkan Sen- Also referred to as the conversion line. This line is the midpoint of the 9 day high-low range. So on a daily chart, its the midpoint of the 9 days high-low average. The calculation is as below:

Conversion Line= (9 period high+9 period low)/2

• Chikou Span- This is a line which tracks the bar close but is plotted 26 bars in the past. So on a chart, the current position of this line indicates the bar close 26 bars ago.

• Senkou Span A- Also referred to as the Leading Span A, this line forms one of the 2 lines which make up the cloud boundaries. The value is the midpoint between the conversion line and base line. This is plotted 26 periods ahead.vThe calculation is as below:

Leading Span A= (conversion line+ base line)/2

• Senkou Span B- Also referred to as Leading Span B, this is the other line which forms the Ichimoku cloud. This line is the average of the 52 period high and low and is plotted 26 periods into the future. The calculation is as below:

Leading Span B= (52 period high+ 52 period low)/2

Before we begin a dive into the specifics of this indicator please note, I'll be using the English names for these lines. Also, if you observe the charts to follow you will notice the following properties which hold true across all instruments;

• The Conversion line is usually the fastest and follows price the most closely. This stands to reason since its the 9 day average.

• The Base line, which is effectively a 26 day moving average is slower than the conversion line but tracks price decently as well.

The chart on the next page illustrates the various lines in play. The cloud itself is denoted with solid black color when the Leading Span A is <u>above</u> Leading Span B and as vertical stripes when Leading Span A is <u>below</u> Leading Span B. The base line and conversion line are presented as thick lines and the Chikou Span as the dotted line.

The Leading Span A and B are sometimes referred to as the Up Kumo and Down Kumo in certain charting software.

Some general trend conclusions can be drawn from a chart with the cloud on it. Prices are considered to be in an uptrend when above the cloud, downtrend when below it and in a range when within it. Further, the uptrend is strengthened when Leading Span A is above Span B, that is, the cloud is filled with vertical stripes as per the previous chart, and the downtrend is strengthened when Span A is below Span B, or the cloud is fully colored as per the previous chart.

The cloud also offers us a support/resistance level as per current price action but also in the future. This is because the entire cloud is plotted forward 26 days and can give us a good glimpse of probable future price action. In general it is important to remember that we ought to favor signals which are in line with the larger trend. That is, we prefer bullish signals when the price is above the cloud and the cloud is filled with stripes (that is, leading span A is above B) and bearish signals when price is below the cloud and is solid in color (that is A is below B). Any counter signals such as a bullish signal when price is below the cloud or span A is below B, is considered weak and I recommend beginners stay away from such signals.

This indicator throws up a variety of signals so let us now look at each one of them in greater detail.

Price/Cloud Crossover Signals

The position of price above or below the cloud, as previously mentioned, indicates or reinforces an existing bullish or bearish trend. Thus it stands to reason that a price crossover of the cloud indicates a trend change and is a reliable entry signal for us. The direction is further enforced due to the cloud being plotted 26 period in the future.

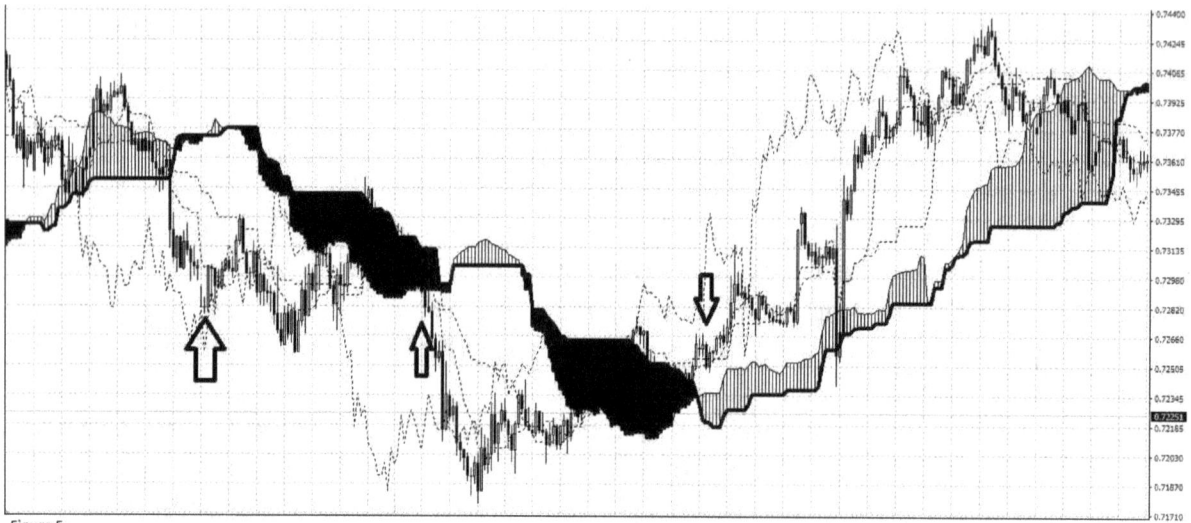

Figure 5

Figure 5 above illustrates how effective the crossover strategy is. The above chart of the NZD/USD fx pair is of the 60 minute timeframe. Notice how when price has multiple closes below the cloud and when the cloud is colored solid, that is, span B is above A, price tends to continue downwards for a while. The same pattern repeats itself on the bullish side as we move towards the right of the chart.

There isn't any fixed rule about how to enter in such situations. If you're following a moving average crossover strategy, then you can use similar entry rules as that. I recommend entering only when price has printed a few bars closing below or above the cloud. A conservative stop placement would be past the top of the Span B in bearish cases and below Span B in bullish cases. You will need to play around with this to see which fits you best since every trader has a different definition of risk. Experiment with it and implement that strategy which makes you the most money on paper.

Chapter 20: CHOOSE THE RIGHT BROKER

Following are a list of things required for becoming a successful Forex trader

Trading plan: A forex trader should have a trading plan that should be prepared well in advance. The trading plan should list out his entry and exit conditions as well as his money management rules. This is of utmost importance and he should religiously follow his trading plan to the tee. In order to become a successful forex trader, he should never deviate from the trading plan.

Discipline: This is one of the most important qualities needed to be a successful forex trader. A trader should be disciplined and methodical in the way he goes about with forex trading. He should not only meticulously plan his trading, but should also be disciplined enough to follow it.

Ability to do analysis: A forex trader should have the ability to analyze the technical charts and other financial data in order to become a successful forex trader. He should invest in himself and learn how to use the financial tools that would help in becoming a better trader. Trading is a very competitive job and one needs to be always one step ahead of others in order to be successful.

Emotional stability: It is very important to keep emotions and trading separate. In order to be successful, the trader should be able to trade like a machine and not let emotions affect his trades. He shouldn't let losses affect him nor should he get overly excited about the winning trades.

Hard work: Nothing beats hard work for becoming a successful forex trader. The trader should be prepared to put in a lot of hours and research the forex market thoroughly before each trading day. Most successful forex traders have a pre-trading session wherein they analyze the global markets, check charts, read various financial newspapers, note down key economic events of the day etc. before they start their trades.

Good knowledge of charting and analysis tools: In order to be a successful forex trader, it is very important to have good knowledge on the usage of charting and other analytic software. The usage of these trading software's raises the odds of success considerably, so it is important to have a good understanding of them.

Constant Learning: Trading field requires constant learning. The trader should be prepared to learn throughout his trading career. Something that might work now might not work after 5 years. So it's very important to constantly adapt and keep learning in order to be a step ahead of others. A good trader should be on the constant look out of learning new things that might help him with his trading be it the usage of a trading software or a new way of analysis.

Mastering fear: It is very important to master fear in order to be a successful forex trader. The trader should be prepared to take losses now and again and should understand that it's a part and parcel of the game. The inability to book losses and holding on to a losing position can result in more losses. The trader should also be ready to take a trade when a good opportunity arises and should not allow fear to hold him back.

Thinking on your own: It is very important to think on your own and make trading decisions and to not just blindly follow the crowd. As the saying goes, "buy into the fear and sell into the greed!" Now, this does not mean to always do the opposite to what others do. It just means that the trader should have an open mind and should have the ability to think on his own and make decisions accordingly.

Awareness of the global events: Forex markets are affected by the major international events that occur. The key economic events happening globally as the forex markets are traded globally and affected by these economic events. A few examples of the key economic events are Federal Bank interest rate decision, ECB rate decision, GDP data of key economies, job data of key economies, inflation data of key economies etc.

Never blame the market: The market might behave irrationally but the trader should be responsible for reading the market cues and making trading decisions. Instead of playing the blame game he should learn from each mistake and learn from it. The trader should understand the risks associated with trading and have a proper money management rule in place.

Trading journal: It is important to maintain a trading journal and make an entry of all the trades he makes. The reasons for taking that particular trade should also be noted down. This would help in analyzing the trades later and help in avoiding the mistakes made. This would also help in identifying the good trades made and look for similar patterns later on.

Choosing the right broker: It is important to choose the right broker. Some of the factors that should be considered while selecting a broker should be a) low brokerage b) fast and reliable trading terminal c) ease of trading and good research and charting software's that the broker provides.

Money management rules: This is perhaps the most important among all things that are mentioned till now. A money management rule is basically the rules that define the maximum loss a trader can afford to take per trade or at a point of time. Most forex traders never risk more than 2- 5 % per trade. They also never risk more than 10-20 % at a particular point across all trades. It is very important to follow these rules; else you run the risk of wiping out your entire trading account in a matter of days, if not hours! It is always better to limit your losses and live to fight another day!

Chapter 21: BASIC AND STRATEGIES FOR FIRST TIME TRADER

The most common forex trading techniques can be categorized into two broad groups: long-term trading and short-term trading. With long-term trading, a trader bases his or her analysis on end-of-day data and charts and can decide to maintain a position for several weeks, or even months. What a long-term trader basically does is monitor the trends. One of the advantages of long-term forex trading is that you wouldn't have to monitor the forex market several times during the day, and you would have to complete a lesser number of trade transactions, which translates to lesser commission fees or charges. Additionally, you would also not need to use elaborate equipment or computer software to help in your trend analysis because you would not really spend a lot of time with the analysis and monitoring of the market trends.

Two of the biggest disadvantages of longer-term trading are the requirement to establish bigger stops and the risk of huge equity swings. As a long-term trader, you will have to be well-capitalized so you can be more primed to face those huge equity swings. Because you will only perform several trade transactions in a month, you need to have a lot of patience, especially during months or weeks when you are on the losing end and you are waiting for the market prices to pick up.

With short-term forex trading, a trader will base his or her analysis on intraday data and information and will usually maintain a forex position for just a couple of days or, at most, up to two weeks. The kind of forex trading that short-term traders do is called "swing trading". There are also traders who perform an even shorter form of forex trading called "day trading," where they aim to earn small profits because of price swings that happen within the day. One of the biggest benefits of short-term trading is that you will be able to take advantage of the numerous trading opportunities that happen every day. When you are able to earn even a small amount of profit every day, you have a lesser chance of experiencing any losing months. You will not have to depend on one or two major forex trades that you perform once a year to earn a profit. The biggest drawback of short-term trading is the higher transaction fees or charges that you would be incurring.

Here are the most common trading techniques you can employ to earn profits from forex trading. Carefully read each one and determine which strategy matches your investment objectives and personality type:

1. Scalping

   The primary objective in the scalping forex strategy is to earn small amounts of profit in frequent intervals from minute price movements that can range from two to ten pips. With scalping, you can enter and exit a particular trade within a couple of minutes, or even mere seconds. The small profits that you earn from scalping can eventually add up to a bigger profit because you will be able to enter into a high number of transactions within a day that can range from twenty to one hundred transactions on average.

Many expert traders consider scalping a very risky forex trading strategy, but the level of risk involved in scalping can vary depending on both the actual time of the day you complete your transactions and the forex market that you use. You are more likely to become successful in scalping during trending conditions, and the most ideal trading time is when the forex market is varying within consolidation patterns. When you want to implement the scalping strategy, you need to make sure that you will be able to react and make decisions in a fast manner so that you can get out of a bad trade as soon as you can with minimal pip loss. Because scalping will allow you to take numerous forex trades within the day, you should take any profit opportunities that are presented to you, even if they are a very small amount. You should not aim for a profit that is outside five to ten pips in order to maximize your efforts in scalping.

2. Intraday Trading

When you implement intraday or day forex trading, you will need to close all your positions before the end of the day. With this strategy, the number of transactions that you will close is expected to be much less than the scalping strategy. You will normally analyze a trade and complete it within a short or medium timeframe that involves charts with a thirty minute to an hour timeframe.

3. Position Trading

With the position trading strategy, the objective is to improve your position size in increments as you observe the market evolution to make sure that you are able to maintain a constant level of risk. This technique is also referred to as "averaging into a position," where you will open a new forex position of a similar size and direction each time the risks of the previous position can already be covered.

Chapter 22: TRADING MISTAKES AND HOW TO AVOID IT

Relying too much

Do not make the mistake of over-relying on someone as that will only end badly for you. You have to make your own choices and remain confident of them. It can be your broker or just a friend or family member. They might give you the wrong advice, and you might end up suffering losses. Before you make any kind of investment, you have to compulsorily do a personal inspection and only then invest in the currencies. It is after all your money that is being invested, and so, you have to be careful about it.

No planning

As an investor, you should always work with a plan. Those that don't work with a plan will end up getting lost. It is the same as a tourist going to a new place without a map. He will obviously get lost. So, in order to avoid such a situation, you have to work as per a plan and avoid falling into unnecessary traps. You will be better prepared to take quick decisions. Now say for example there is an opportunity for you to buy a lucrative pair. But just as soon as you buy it you hear that the currency value is going to drop. Here, you have not planned the buying, and so your investment has the chance of going bad. So, to avoid any such issues you should have a plan in place.

Short selling

The next don't of forex is selling short. Selling short refers to you settling for a loss in order to quickly sell off a certain currency. This will only cause you to undergo unnecessary loss. Short selling is not advisable for any trader unless the situation absolutely calls for it. But situations rarely arise, and so, you have to remain patient and wait for the prices to rise again before selling off your currencies.

Picking extremes

Some people make the mistake of picking two extreme currency pairs. That will seem like a good idea but really is not. Say for example you pick a strong currency like the Dollar and a weak one like the Indian rupee. You will have the chance to make a big profit from these no doubt, but you have to calculate the risk that such an investment might put forth. The currency market is extremely volatile, and you have to account for all those things that can go wrong. Being prepared is key, and you have to be as careful as possible while choosing your currency pairs. Stick with the ones that are working well for you and don't experiment too much with it.

Getting emotional

Some traders make the mistake of getting very emotional with their currencies and getting too attached. If that happens, then you will not be able to sell it on time and remain with a profit. You have to trade with your mind and not from your heart. If you think that that is what is happening with you, then you must take stock of the situation at the earliest and fix the problem. Think of currencies as nothing but money making instruments and not any kind of person. Even if a certain currency has worked well for you in the past and is now doing badly, then you have to let go of it and move to another one.

Depending on luck

Do not over depend on your luck. Some people make the mistake of depending too much on their luck and end up making mistakes. Maybe you did well at the beginning owing to beginners luck, and the same might not continue for long. You have to try and remain as practical and logical as possible when you invest in the stock market, and the same extends to your forex investments.

Expecting too much

Do not expect overnight riches with your forex investments. That has never happened and never will. You have to have practical and reasonable expectations if you wish to make it big in the world of forex. Try to remain as practical as possible and think before reaching any consensus.

These form the various dos and don'ts of forex that you have to follow if you wish to make it big.

CONCLUSION

The forex market is a complex world, and everyone is trying to look for the goose that lays the golden egg. In this case, we are talking about that one trade that will simply propel someone to new heights.

People imagine that getting into the forex market is easy, that pretty soon they will be diving into cash the way Scrooge McDuck takes a joyful dive in his pile of gold coins. That rarely happens. But the prospect of making some incredible profits still exists, provided you are ready to navigate the complexities of the forex market.

In fact, here is something you should know.

This is a real market. It is the largest financial market in the world, and you have to treat it as such. You can trade this market part-time, or you can do it every day. In fact, you can make it your business — the business of trading.

People have actually quit their day jobs to get into the world of forex trading. However, that is something that you should not even consider if you are starting out. Do not make rash decisions in the hope that you are going to master the markets and strike rich in no time. Those are wonderful ambitions but are not backed by experience.

You see, trading can be learned, of course, but the experience can't be transmitted.

It has to be constructed by every individual through a personal effort of understanding and hard work.

Another thing that is important to understand is that you will never ever stop learning. Markets are changing every day, and the forex is a living organism that evolves in the same way as all its traders. Always remember that although it seems to be an unknown entity, at the end of the day, the market is merely made up of investors, large and small, from all corners of the world, each with his or her own emotions, psychology, and predictable behaviors and reactions.

Do you ever walk up to a doctor and ask him or her if there is a shortcut to reaching where he or she has reached? Would you do that to an engineer or a renowned sportsperson? These people have developed their skills over time. They have honed their abilities as much as possible before they could use them fluently.

It is the same with the forex market. You might need to put in your efforts to learn the tricks of the trade (no pun intended).

Learn to move on after losses. Don't dwell on missed trades or missed pips after you decide to close. There will be hundreds of opportunities in the future. Follow your plan, and follow your system. Practice every day, and experience will come with time, patience, and discipline. Don't look outside for what's already inside. Leave your ego behind; be humble and smart. You can't decide where the market will go, so learn to see where it wants to lead you, not the other way around. Exit bad trades, and hold on to good trades. Set yourself a goal and stop trading when you have reached it.

www.ingramcontent.com/pod-product-compliance
Lightning Source LLC
Chambersburg PA
CBHW081824200326
41597CB00023B/4378